COURAGEOUS
CURIOSITY

Find Answers Where
Everyone Else is
Afraid to Look

TRAVIS COURNOYER

2 4 6 8 10 9 7 5 3 1

ISBN 979-8-9997762-0-4 (Paperback)

ISBN 979-8-9997762-1-1 (Ebook)

ISBN 979-8-9997762-2-8 (Hardcover)

Published by Ask Anyway LLC
Hawthorne, CA

First Edition: November 2025
Printed in United States of America

Copy editing by Keidi Keating

Cover Design and Interior Typesetting by
FOGLIO | CUSTOM BOOK SPECIALISTS
Body set in *Adobe Garamond Pro* 12pt
Titles set in *Century Gothic* 22pt

FOGLIOPRINT.COM

Dedicated to every stupid question stuck in your throat, waiting for your courage to catch up.

COURAGEOUS CURIOSITY

Find Answers Where Everyone Else is *Afraid to Look*

THE FEAR OF ASKING IS WHAT KEEPS US STUCK, NOT THE FEAR OF NOT KNOWING.

1

THE FEAR

The most beautiful thing in the world hides inside a six-word question. We don't always catch it. Sometimes we dismiss it. But when we're in the room and someone dares to ask it, we feel it.

It's raw. Bare. Human. It's more than a mere question. It's a flare. One that says: *I don't know, but I want to.*

For most of my life, I've been afraid to ask this question. Maybe I was in a room where I was "supposed to already know." Or I worried someone had already asked it, and I missed the answer. Or it was *one of those questions,* the kind you're not supposed to say out loud. And every time, I felt it: that invisible hand, pressing my arm down, telling me, *Don't.*

As I got older, that pressure became heavier. And what started as a small nudge became a weight on my chest, on my shoulders. Pinning me in place, whispering, *Stay quiet. Stay small. Just nod like you get it. It doesn't matter if you do.*

Does this sound familiar?

Have you ever had a burning question, for the air to get *sucked* out of the room as soon as you tried to ask it?

Have you ever felt your face flush and your stomach twist while your mind spiraled? *Don't ask. You'll look like an idiot.* Have you ever asked it anyway and gotten laughed at? Or heard, "That's common knowledge"?

After a while, did that fear start to feel normal?

We're told this fear isn't real. That we should just ignore it. That it doesn't exist. And if you're anything like me, that story started back in Kindergarten.

I can still see Mrs. Pennington, crouched in front of me with those kind, patient eyes. "You can ask anything. There's no such thing as a stupid question."

I believed her. I felt bold. And I still believe her ... kind of.

But adults lie to kids sometimes. My parents did. Yet even now, thirty years later, I can still picture Mrs. Pennington's eyes, steady and sure. And I *want* to believe her.

The memory of Mrs. Pennington reminds me of other things I'd been *told* about as a kid. About other people who—to my vulnerable, naive mind—were just as kind.

Like Santa.

I vividly remember what it felt like to believe in him. That he was going to bring presents. I remember waiting by my door on Christmas Eve, peeking through the crack, desperate to catch him. Falling asleep on the floor from sheer effort, and waking up to magic.

But I also remember the day it shattered.

It was a few days before Christmas. While riding in the back of my dad's truck, I found a weird tube with little metal-rubber things. At the time, I didn't think much of it. I just put it back. Then Christmas morning came. I unwrapped a present from Santa—and there it was. The same tube. I looked more closely at it; brushes for my drum kit.

I stared at my parents, confused.

They just smiled. "How did Santa *know* that's what you wanted?"

That was it. The moment my world broke open. Not just Santa. Not just that one lie. No, something bigger clicked into place, and I realized that even the people I love the most will lie to me.

I bet you have a story like that too. A moment you caught someone in a lie, and it changed your world. A parent. A teacher. An uncle. Someone trying to soften a blow.

I was aways going to figure out Santa wasn't real. Someone would have told me eventually. But that doesn't change the fact that lies, even the ones meant to shield us, can hurt if we believe them too long.

So here's my question: If we know that, why do we still tell people *stupid questions don't exist*?

Why do we keep whispering that if we feel fear, it's our fault? That we need to try to be stronger—need to avoid that fear?

Even the most brilliant minds echo the same belief. Carl Sagan wrote it in *The Demon-Haunted World*: "Every question is a cry to understand the world. There is no such thing as a dumb question."

I respect Carl Sagan. Deeply. But that's not my truth. And it might not be yours, either. Sometimes, the people we trust the most hand us a version of the world that's not the whole truth.

Because stupid questions *do* exist. I've asked plenty. So have you. So has every person you know. Even your Kindergarten teacher. And yes, even Carl Sagan. But asking a stupid question doesn't make you stupid. It makes you *brave*.

Because sometimes it's *scary* to ask. That fear—the heat in your cheeks, the knot in your stomach, the sting when someone dismisses you—that's not a sign you're an idiot. It's a sign of courage. It's proof of your vulnerability and humanity. Proof you're willing to admit, *I don't know, but I want to.*

> Stupid people don't ask stupid
> questions. Courageous people do.

It doesn't matter if you've asked the wrong thing at the wrong time. It doesn't matter if it's something you "should have known." It matters that you asked to begin with, and that you'll ask again and again and keep seeking answers.

> A stupid question is only stupid because
> of the shame the asker feels, whether
> before, during, or after asking.

It doesn't even have to be spoken aloud. In fact, the ones we *don't* ask, that we keep bottled up, are the most dangerous. They fester. The unspoken question poisons us quietly. It takes strength for us to walk through that shame. To drag that question into the light. To say, *I need help*, even while your throat is closing up from fear.

We've all been lying. Not just to our kids, but to ourselves. Every time we say stupid questions don't exist, we erase the courage it takes to ask them. The courage needed to ask is real. And so are the people who feel that tug every time they want to raise their hand.

Yes, there are times when it's *easy* to ask. Maybe in Kindergarten, where teachers *fight so hard* to shut down any shame as soon as it appears. Or maybe if you're the next Carl Sagan—by the time he wrote that book, perhaps he truly wasn't afraid to ask anything. But stupid questions will always exist for me. And if you're here, reading this, I bet they exist for you too.

I wrote this book for two reasons.

First, because I needed to. Some of the stupid questions I've asked—and the places they've taken me—have left me buried in shame. Shame I never told anyone about. Until now. But now, I want to raise my hand and say them out loud, hoping it'll help you feel less alone and maybe even willing to raise your hand, too.

Second, I want to open a door. The one that's been shut by teachers and parents and mentors and heroes who all meant well. They told us stupid questions don't exist. And we believed them because it felt safer that way.

But not only do stupid questions exist, I can define them.

A stupid question is any honest question
you're shamed for asking

That's the heartbeat of this book. A clear understanding that stupid questions circle shame. Because when we name something, we can work with it. And when we work with it, we can build. We can build a new world. One where courage beats silence. Where every honest question, no matter how clumsy or raw, is welcomed, not swatted away. A world where we ask that question to others instead of hiding it.

Here's how the book unfolds: I'll tell you stories, times I asked stupid questions. Each story starts with the question itself, no context, just like the person hearing it from me first encountered it. Then I'll take you behind the scenes to reveal the shame that shaped the question.

After each group of questions, we'll pause to unpack the commonalities linking the group together through this new lens. That's it. We'll keep doing that, ping-pong between stories and reflection, connecting dots so we don't get lost. A group of four stories with four stupid questions, one moment of reflection. That's how we practice: learn, stumble, reflect, repeat. It's the same cycle it takes to build lasting curiosity with courage.

We'll begin at rock bottom, the darkest moment of my life. Where fear and shame pinned me down so hard, I never talked about it. For ten years. Where a single stupid question eventually cracked things open just enough to let in a sliver of light when I needed it most.

I didn't know it yet, but that question? It saved me.

From there, we'll walk through the messy middle, rebuilding from the ground up, tripping forward and finding my footing. You'll see how stupid questions kept showing up. Sharper. Heavier. More powerful. And how they started to lead me somewhere new. You'll sit with me in basements, open offices, and small conference rooms, places where I found my way because I asked the question nobody else wanted to. You'll watch me crumble under shame, then learn how to name it. You'll watch me succeed in ways that astound. You'll see me fail. Spectacularly. And get back up again.

I won't hold back. I'll lay it all bare for you to pick it apart. Then, by the end, your own questions will want to break free. And you'll be the one with a choice.

You can either believe what the world told you, that *stupid questions don't exist*. Or you can choose something better. Something real. Something beautiful. You can choose to ask someone.

And, before you do, you can preface with the bravest, most beautiful question in the world. To remind yourself, *I am courageous. I am worth asking.* Even if it's going to be messy.

"Can I ask a stupid question?"

A SINGLE STUPID QUESTION IS ALL IT TAKES TO START RESHAPING YOUR LIFE.

2 THE QUESTION

"Do you think it could work?"

The words spilled out before I could catch them. I tried to make it sound like just another in the long line of questions I'd lobbed across my advisor's desk before. But this one simple question would change everything.

It was 2014, and Reno was buried under snow and ice. I had this nagging idea for a new research project so simple, it felt idiotic to even bring up. But I couldn't let it go. So I asked, half-hoping my advisor would laugh, or shake their head, or at least tell me why it was a dead end.

Instead, they just shrugged. "It's possible," they said. "The reagents are cheap, and we already have them in the lab. Why don't you go ahead and try it? Let me know how it goes."

That was it. No fanfare. No fireworks.

I should've felt relieved. I'd spent days working up the nerve to ask, turning it over and over in my head, trying to convince myself it was okay to risk looking stupid. To risk wasting my advisor's time. And now that I had the green light, tension should have melted away. But it didn't. Instead, I felt like I'd just stepped into a void. A wide, empty space with no clear path forward.

And that, I realized, was exactly why I needed this little experiment to work. Because outside the lab, my whole life was barely holding together.

I'd hit a new low. I was living in the worst house you can imagine. The kind you only agree to rent when the price is so low, it feels like a trap. The landlord was mid-renovation, but in the meantime, the house was a wreck. I lived in the basement, and the only light came from a single bare bulb in the hallway. To stretch that one bit of light as far as I could, I'd taken the doors off the bathroom, bedroom, and kitchen, just so the glow could bleed into every room. And the shower? No curtain. No rod to hang one from, either. So if I wanted a warm shower, I had to crouch against the wall so the water wouldn't splash onto the floor. And that was when the hot water worked at all.

The night before I asked my advisor the question that would change everything, I was making Mac 'n Cheese in my gloomy little kitchen when something scraped across the floor. From the corner of my eye, there was a blur of movement, too fast to catch. Too big to be a mouse, whatever it was ran right between my legs and under the sink.

I was on the phone with Emily when it happened, this amazing new girl I'd just started seeing. I yelped, even though I tried to play it cool. She asked what happened, and I paused for too long.

She laughed, and said, only half-joking, "Look, you don't have to tell me. But I'm never coming over there again."

My heart rate was still high, but her understanding helped to calm me down a little. And I couldn't help but think, *Man, she's a keeper.*

I put the bedroom door back on the hinges that night and ate my dinner by candlelight. I studied some scientific papers for the rest of the evening, trying not to think about the creature in the kitchen.

I told myself I could live with it, but those years were a lot harder than I'd imagined.

In college, chemistry had clicked for me. I barely had to try. I filled my days with clubs, sports, jobs, and parties. I was a machine living for the hustle, measuring my worth by how much I crammed into each day. But grad school was a totally different beast. I won't say it was indentured servitude, but if you were to say it, I wouldn't argue.

The first few months lulled me into thinking I could handle it; ski trips, parties, late nights that still felt optional. But by the time I stood in my advisor's doorway asking this question, everything had changed.

Fourteen-hour days in the lab? Standard. Skipping meals just to grab ten extra minutes with a test setup? Expected. Six days a week in the lab, the seventh curled up with papers at the rat house? Routine. The only real break I had was slamming back enough alcohol fast enough to keep my brain from spinning out.

Focus. That was the only thing that mattered.

And honestly, I didn't even fully clock what the question about trying this experiment meant or how much it might change things. I was too busy obsessing over how dumb it sounded.

I was sure my advisor would laugh at me. Point out something obvious

I'd missed. I was terrified they'd think I was wasting their time. Worse, I was scared I *was* wasting their time. I kept telling myself it was just a simple question. But that's the lie. The real danger isn't in asking, but in believing that simple questions exist at all.

> There's no such thing as a simple question. Every question—every single one—is packed with invisible weight.

Every question is stitched out of hopes, doubts, fears, and the fragile parts of ourselves we try so hard to hide. Even the ones that sound easy. Sometimes, *especially* those ones.

But I hadn't learned that. Not yet. So, I asked. And I got my answer.

No applause. No epiphany. Just quiet permission, and the beginning of everything that followed.

SOME QUESTIONS BUILD A BRIDGE FORWARD. OTHERS LIGHT THE BRIDGE ON FIRE.

3

THE RISK

"Do you think I should?" I asked.

Up until that moment, I'd felt nothing but momentum. But suddenly, my chest tightened. It should have felt thrilling. Instead, it felt like freefall.

It had been about a month since I first stumbled into the idea. A month since I'd asked that first stupid question. A month since it blasted everything wide open. And there I was again, standing in my advisor's doorway. Only, this time, my heart was racing as everything sped up around me: too fast to process, too fast to breathe.

My advisor had just floated the biggest invitation of my life: Present my new research project—the same little experiment that had skyrocketed in ways I never imagined—at the American Chemical Society conference. The national stage. Every chemist went. The problem was, the deadline to apply as a presenter was noon the next day.

I had no time to weigh it. No time to second-guess. But still, I froze.

What started as a five-minute setup and a single sharp observation had lit up like a flare.

My advisor didn't believe me, until they saw it for themselves. That look. That spark. We both knew. We weren't just tinkering anymore. We'd discovered something. A hole in the wall. And through that hole? Something new. Uncharted, uncertain, unpredictable. A scientist's dream.

If I was right—if everything I believed about this reaction held up—this was beyond a solid thesis. I was staring down a shot at a career I hadn't even dared dream about. But if I was wrong? Or if even a single thread came loose? It would just be a mess with my name on it. My mistake. My fallout.

Deciding whether to stand on that stage would be a bet. A big one. If it all held together, my advisor would be credited as a trailblazer, the one who thought to look here for this new field. And sure, I'd ride the wave too. But if it fell apart? Someone with more resources and sharper tools would have the opportunity to swoop in, stitch up the gaps, and publish it first. And we'd be left in the dust. My advisor would be branded the fool. And I'd just … disappear.

I still had *so much* work left to do. So many questions remained unanswered. And no money to chase them with. No fancy equipment. No big budget. Just me, some glassware, a fragile idea hanging by a thread, and someone else's reagents.

Emily had already asked me to stop bringing work home. Watching me burn out in real time wasn't exactly her idea of intimacy. Which is why I stood in that doorway, staring at my advisor instead, every nerve on edge and grasping for something solid.

"Do you think I should?"

The smile they returned was small. Measured. Calm. "If *you* think we're ready," the words came out slowly, "then *I* think we are, too." It was quiet. Simple. But it landed like a hammer. The kind of answer that slides a key across the table and says, this is yours now. Your choice.

I took a breath, just long enough to fake confidence. "Okay. Let's do it. I'll pull together the figures and draft the presentation!"

They nodded slowly. "Then okay."

And right there, between the nod and their okay, I felt it. The full burden being placed gently on my back. And I knew that if it succeeded, my advisor would be the name everyone remembered. This wasn't a shared risk. It was mine alone.

I should have seen it coming. I should have known better than to say yes. Everyone had warned me. *Keep your guard up. Don't lose yourself in the work.*

There were stories. One about a Harvard chem graduate student who took his own life in the 90s and named his advisor in the note. But I'd brushed it off. Figured I was different. Tougher. So I never asked the harder question: *What if both things were true? What if the system is broken, and it can break me too?* But there was no time to think about any of that now. The decision was made. My decision. And as soon as my advisor said "okay," a metaphorical door slammed shut behind me. I was locked in. This was happening.

"The deadline's noon tomorrow," they continued. "Get me a draft of the abstract tonight so I'll have time to review it?"

I stumbled back to the lab and stared at my screen. My hands shook as I tapped out the first few lines, erasing and rewriting before anything even made sense. I was terrified. But I was too far in to back out.

I'd read once, that our bodies process fear the same way they process excitement. So I told myself, *You're not scared. You're excited. This is good.* Hoping—begging—that if I said it enough, I might start to believe it. But I couldn't. It wasn't working.

So I asked the nearest person for help. A more senior grad student in the same lab. It was the wrong question, but I asked all the same. I asked if they had an abstract template I could use, and when I explained why I needed it, their eyebrows shot up. They tilted their head, eyes narrowed as if I'd just announced I was about to skydive without a parachute.

"You're sure about that? Didn't you *just* start that project?"

I wasn't sure. Not even close. But instead of admitting it, I dug in. I told myself the story I needed to hear. That it was fine. That I had the main data and just needed a summary. Just bullet points. And the rest would be filled in later.

I smiled. Shrugged. And I gave the same answer every overworked twenty-something gives before doing something wildly reckless. "It'll be fine."

The template landed in my inbox. And it was too late to back out now.

So, I got to work.

SOME QUESTIONS LEAVE A SCAR.

4

THE FALL

What if I just quit?

I was back in the chemistry department doorway again. Three days prior, I'd stood on a national stage. Now, I stood here, shaking and sobbing.

The two months that led to this moment had unraveled into outright disaster. And somewhere along the way, I'd lost my grip on the hope that had carried me this far. Maybe I wasn't cut out for this. Maybe I wasn't just failing. Maybe I was failing *spectacularly*. And, worst of all, maybe I was getting what I deserved.

It'd started almost immediately after I'd agreed to present. I ran a critical test expecting a clear, obvious result and got the exact opposite. I'd stared at the numbers, willing them to change, to mean something different. It was unsettling.

When I'd showed my advisor, they'd shrugged and said, "Try it again. Maybe recalibrate the instrument."

So I did. Only to get the same result.

I'd dismantled the instrument. Cleaned its sensors. Ran every diagnostic I could think of. Then I'd reran the test.

Same result. Only this time, it was even more obvious and impossible to misread.

Cleaning the sensors hadn't fixed the mistake. It'd only made my incorrect hypothesis harder to ignore.

So I did what any scientist is supposed to do in times like these. I'd dug in. I'd doubled down. I'd read every paper, every citation, every reference that even touched this corner of chemistry. And over and over, they pointed to what *should* have happened. Not what had.

If I'd agreed with what the data was *actually* saying, then I would have to accept that everyone, not just me, was wrong. And I didn't want to do that.

Chemists love a challenge. But not *that* kind of challenge. I didn't want to stand against every other chemist alive.

I'd reran the experiment. Same result. I'd swapped out the reagents for fresh ones. Same result. I'd cleaned everything again and again, until my hands were raw. Still, the same damn result.

I'd started running a whole suite of tests every time I'd touched that five-minute experiment. Each round took two full days. And with each failure, the conference loomed closer.

Two weeks before the conference, I'd finally given up. I'd stopped trying to fix it. I'd stopped trying to explain it. Instead, I'd decided to present everything I had—the good, the bad, the parts that didn't fit—and just … accept it. If I'd fail, I'd at least do so with unwavering confidence. But the discrepancy was still there. I'd just buried it in the fine print and softened it with words so gentle, you'd think I was describing a sunrise, not a flaw.

I'd yanked my laptop out as soon as the plane had taken off for the conference, frantically reviewing how the slides were edited to strike the perfect balance between having the data there but making it impossible to see. I'd hid my failure as best as I could. I'd told myself it would be fine. I'd told myself I could fake it just long enough to survive the talk. But I knew the truth. I was terrified.

There were maybe two hundred people in the room when I'd walked up onto the stage.

I'd shaken so badly, I could barely hold the clicker. I'd spoken so fast, my forty-minute talk was over in twenty. It'd felt like a snake had wrapped itself around my heart, squeezing tighter with every word while a gorilla had jumped on my back and pulled my shoulders backward, tearing me apart.

I'd finished speaking and stood there, waiting. Praying. But nothing happened. No hands were raised. No questions asked. Just a room full of kind, tired smiles. The tension had slowly started to ease as I'd looked around. Maybe, somehow, I'd made it through. Maybe nobody noticed. Maybe—

"Okay, well if there are no questions, I'd like to ask one." My advisor's voice had cut through the air like a whip. "Can you explain the discrepancy on slide 17? Doesn't that result disagree with your main hypothesis?"

They'd said it with a calm, curious smile, like they were seeing this for the first time. Like we hadn't spent two months agonizing over it together.

The snake had returned. The gorilla, too. Only this time, they'd crushed harder.

Without any other option, I'd given an honest answer. I'd explained in detail why the result was the opposite of what had been expected and finished with, "the way you know this is new, is because all existing understanding of this chemistry disagrees with this result. Nothing we know today explains it."

The room had frozen. Smiles had vanished. Faces had turned down.

And then—to make it worse—the conference leader had stepped up to the mic. "Well, since we're done early, we'll just … pause here to stay on schedule."

I had to stand there on that stage shaking and alone, with the weight of two hundred silent stares pressing down on me.

What had cut the deepest wasn't the embarrassment. It was that my advisor had known. We'd dissected every slide together. We'd talked about the discrepancy for weeks. It hadn't just been me who didn't have an answer. My advisor hadn't either.

In the weeks leading up to the conference, I'd only been given one instruction: "You can't present that result alongside your hypothesis. You need a new one, or you need data that backs up your hypothesis."

Every time I'd asked for help, every time I'd asked, "Okay, so what hypothesis should I present then? What could possibly explain this?" the answer was the same.

"Figure it out."

No help. No guidance. Just a command tossed over a shoulder like I wasn't even worth turning around for.

I never, not once, expected them to turn around and use it against me. Not like this. Not on a national stage. It wasn't just a question my advisor had asked that day. It was a public execution delivered with a smile.

Three days later, I was back in the chemistry building. Same hallway. Same beat-up notebook. The same voice tearing into me. My advisor yelled, loud enough that people in the hallway could probably hear, but I don't remember all the words. I remember "embarrassment." I remember "failure." I remember a blotch of ink spread across my notebook and realizing, vaguely, that I was crying. But even then, through the shaking and the shame, some part of me still scrambled for a solution.

Maybe if I apologized. Maybe if I rewrote the talk. Maybe if I issued a correction to the conference committee. Maybe—

"Why don't you go cry to your girlfriend about it? Come back when you're ready to work."

I froze. My nervous system didn't know what to do; cry, run, collapse. Before I could stop myself, a small, broken, "okay" slipped out. And I waited. For something. A plan. A scrap of advice. A hug. Anything. But my advisor turned to their keyboard, fingers clacking like I'd never been there.

That was it. The conversation was over.

As I staggered away from the doorway back to the lab, my mind flooded with "it's my fault" and thoughts about that Harvard student. And the warnings. Had he stood in a doorway, too? Shaking and crying? Still trying to believe he could fix it?

What if I just quit?

The ground lurched sideways. My chest pulled in tight. My stomach twisted. My legs wobbled. I barely caught myself on the lab door's handle. I was falling, harder and faster than I'd ever fallen before.

THERE'S
ALWAYS A
PART OF YOU
THAT STILL
WANTS TO
TRY. ALL YOU
HAVE TO DO
IS LISTEN
FOR IT.

5 THE SPARK

"Is it really that simple?" I said to the empty room, tears of joy welling.

I hadn't left my bed in days. Classes? Missed them. The chemistry department? Avoided like the plague. Even Emily, patient as she was, couldn't find her way in. I just stared at the ceiling, willing myself to disappear. At some point, I'd turned on a movie, but I don't remember picking it. I just needed something—*anything*—to drown out the silence.

A week had crawled by since that last conversation with my now-former advisor.

Less than twenty-four hours after being told to go cry to my girlfriend, I'd cleared out my things from the lab. I left no trace behind, only a resignation letter on an empty desk.

Every grad student who'd warned me could have said, "I told you so." None of them did. Instead, there'd been quiet looks. Small nods. They'd asked, "Are you okay?" Their concern hadn't been for my career but for me. And it made sense. A year and a half into my PhD, I was back at zero. If I'd stayed and started over, they'd reminded me, it could take seven years or more before I finished.

If I'd stayed. If I could.

The part that scared me most wasn't starting over. It was that there was no one left to start with. Inorganic chemistry had always been my home. But there were only two other professors in that building who worked in that field, and neither one was looking for a new graduate student. And without an advisor, you can't get a PhD. No matter how hard you work. No matter how much you want it. Which meant my choices were simple. And awful.

I could quit the PhD program altogether. Or I could switch specialties. Start from scratch, truly.

I knew it. I knew how bad it was. But somehow, that wasn't even the part that hurt the most. I couldn't stop beating myself up over the first-year student I'd convinced to join my former advisor's lab. I'd promised I would be there. That I'd pave the way for their success. That I'd be there to support their PhD no matter what. But in the end, I'd done to them exactly what my former advisor had done for me. Only difference was, I'd given up and left.

I'd abandoned that grad student. While my advisor hadn't given up on me even after everything I'd done to embarrass them in front of a national audience. So as bad as I was feeling about what had happened to me, I'd done something even worse to someone else. And the shame of that dragged me somewhere darker than I'd ever been before.

I'm not talking about the darkness in that poorly lit house basement. By this point, the landlord had actually installed lighting in every room. I even had a shower curtain. Ironically, while my life fell apart around me, the house I was in continually got better as the landlord marched steadily through his renovation.

Figures.

No, what had shattered was something deep inside me. I'd always told myself I was a great chemist. A great mentor. But with so much of my identity tied to my PhD, and the promises I'd made, I started questioning whether either were true. No matter what happened, I would always be the kid who'd failed the person who trusted him. Who'd failed his advisor. Who'd made promises and broke them.

Maybe I wasn't smart. Maybe I wasn't a good mentor. Maybe I wasn't cut out for this PhD thing at all.

I dragged myself through the week, hollow and aimless. Life drifted past, like I was sealed underneath glass. Nothing seemed to matter anymore. I lost my phone for two days, but I hardly noticed. All the fire that had once burned inside me was gone. All the beautiful things I'd dreamed of doing for the world felt impossibly far away.

So there I was. Lying in bed. Staring blankly at a movie I didn't even remember choosing, ping-ponging back and forth between two impossible options: I could quit and disappear; or I could stay and suffocate. For years.

Could I even walk into that department again knowing I'd have to see the student I'd abandoned? Could I even breathe the same air as my former advisor?

The pain made more sense the longer I sat in it. That Harvard student had seen it clearly. Maybe he'd been braver than me. Maybe I should just—

Then, she started singing. The girl in the movie. She spun a castle out of ice with the wave of a hand. She built something beautiful from nothing but who she was. Who she'd always been. And then, she said it, those three words that broke the silence *just* long enough for me to breathe again:

"Let it go."

It hit me like a jolt of electricity.

What I'd mistaken for gravity—something holding me down—suddenly felt like something else entirely. Not a heavy weight. Just ... a pull. As if the pressure had been trying to move me, not stop me.

The thoughts flooded in.

I hadn't started my PhD to impress anyone. Not any students I'd made promises to. Not two hundred random people. Not that advisor. Not even myself. I'd started it because I love chemistry. Because even when everything else was crumbling, I still wanted to know why molecules dance the way they do. That was me. That had always been me. And I wasn't going to quit. I wasn't going to run two-thousand miles away back to Rhode Island. Because I loved Emily. Because I loved this work. Because if anything was going to define me now, it wasn't going to be my failure. It would be all of the things I loved. It would be the next experiment. The next question. The next idea.

"Is it really that simple?"

After a moment of hesitation, I let myself believe it. The river of tears came. And as they poured out, the vigor of life poured back in. I wiped my face and let out a breath I hadn't realized I was holding.

I'd lost a week. Fine. But I wasn't out yet. I had a fifty-fifty chance. Two professors, and I only needed one. That was an easy problem.

Oh, and maybe I should call Emily and finally admit I love her. First things first.

THE STUPID QUESTION WAS NEVER THE DANGER. IT WAS ALWAYS THE WAY OUT.

THE DOOR

What does it really mean to hit rock bottom? Economists in the 1860s used the phrase first as the firm bottom of an economic system. A place solid enough to rebuild from. Geologists meant it more literally; bedrock. The unshakable layer beneath the shifting soil. But over time, "rock bottom" lost its hopeful edge. It stopped being about something solid in favor of being about how far you could fall before you disappeared.

I know that feeling. Maybe you do too? If you're unsure, here's how I define it: *Rock bottom is the overwhelming gap between where you are and the support you need to survive.* It's about how impossible it feels to climb back up from wherever we've fallen. At least, that's how it felt when I was laying in bed that week quietly contemplating suicide.

There are plenty of books about rock bottom. They tell the big stories, the 8-mile deep struggles, homelessness, addiction, life-threatening illness, financial ruin. These stories matter because they prove one crucial thing: even from the darkest places, recovery is possible. No matter how deep the hole, you *can* reach your way out.

But…taking the first step, no matter how deep the hole you find yourself in? Simple: ask one stupid question. One tiny, terrifying moment of brazen honesty. And finding the courage to ask it—out loud—*because* you're afraid of asking it.

But what is that question? For you, personally? It could be anything that provides answers for your specific situation and struggle. It could be, "Am I an alcoholic?" "Do I actually want this?" Or even, "Do you still love me?"

> The terrifying part isn't the question itself but knowing that once you ask it, an answer will come. And when it does, everything changes.

When I quit my first advisor's research group, I let the fear run circles in my head. *Quit or die. Quit or die.* Either way, I'd be admitting failure. Either way, I wouldn't be who I thought I was supposed to be. And the loop kept spinning until I stopped fighting it. Until I finally asked the only question that mattered.

The stupid question I finally asked was, "Will this define me?"

The days I spent spiraling were just me trying to find the question hiding underneath it all. Did I really think my life had so little value that one failure meant it wasn't worth living anymore? When framed that way, the answer's obvious. Of course not. I was earning a PhD in America. I had a family that loved me. I had work I was proud of. I even loved Reno. And I was dating a woman who, for some reason I still couldn't fathom, hadn't given up on me despite my best efforts to destroy it all. There were thousands of reasons to keep going. And the moment I found the right question—the moment I actually said it out loud—the answer was obvious.

The choices hadn't been *quit* or *die*. They were quit, die, or *try again*.

If I'd believed that stupid questions don't exist, I never would have found that answer. I would have thought I was stupid for even needing to ask. But it's not stupid to ask. It's not a sign of weakness. It's simply … human. It's wired into us from the beginning.

You, dear reader, were born insatiably curious. You were born with questions no one had time to answer. A child's unabashed curiosity might be the most beautiful thing in the universe. That's why asking a stupid question in your darkest moments is so powerful. It reconnects you to that version of yourself, the gloriously, insatiably curious person you used to be. The one who didn't know fear yet. The one who asked without shame.

There's a problem separating us from our former gloriously curious selves, though. At about the same time we take the training wheels off our kids' bikes, we strap metaphorical training wheels onto their curiosity instead. We start teaching them when it's "safe" to ask and when it's "smart" to stay quiet. And, without meaning to, we slow them down. Committing to asking stupid questions honestly and openly is like taking the training wheels back off. It lets you move faster. It lets you go farther. But it also means you're more likely to fall, at least until you regain your balance.

My own collapse serves as a perfect example. The career path my advisor had mapped out for me wasn't actually the path I'd been meant to walk. And it took asking stupid questions—four of them, and many more after—to eventually lead me somewhere I was *actually* meant to go.

> Marching through your shame to ask
> stupid questions reconnects you to the
> natural curiosity you were born with.

Connecting to your childlike curiosity can move mountains. But it can also dig up stuff you've buried. That's the thing about stupid questions. Sure, they offer new answers. But they also surface old wounds. And sometimes, the answer you get isn't clarity. It's grief. But that's where forgiveness sneaks in, at the very start of it.

> Forgiveness is part of the first step to
> climb out of rock bottom.

And as Brené Brown, a researcher best known for her work on shame and vulnerability, quotes in her book *Rising Strong*, "In order for forgiveness to happen, something has to die. If you make a choice to forgive, you have to face into the pain. You simply have to hurt."

She's right. Because to ask the real stupid question, to say it out loud, is to let go of who you thought you were and what you thought you deserved. It's the beginning of everything that comes next.

So yes, the first step is a question. But often, you can't even take that step until forgiveness has played a part. You have to forgive someone for something. Sometimes it's someone else. Sometimes it's yourself. It's probably yourself, most often. And some days, the weight of that is too much.

If you're too exhausted to even find the question, start simpler. Find someone you trust. Look them in the eye and say, "Can I ask you a stupid question?" Their answer doesn't matter. Just start talking. The question will find its way to you. It always does. All you have to do is forgive yourself for needing to ask, then *ask anyway*. Open the door, and step through.

Stupid questions have always been powerful. But power cuts both ways. For centuries, stupid questions have been used to embarrass, to silence, to shame. And somewhere along the way, we forgot they were meant for something better. A stupid question was never meant to be a weapon. It was supposed to be a way forward.

Asking one, even when it feels foolish, is a deliberate act of defiance. It's a refusal to let shame decide who we are or what happens next. It's what separates the people who stay stuck from the ones who move forward. And the ones who ask anyway, those are the people I call Courageously Curious.

Over the past ten years, life has taught me one brutal lesson over and over again: *It's easy to say you'll ask. It's a lot harder to open your mouth and let the question come out.* You have to keep asking through fair weather and foul. You have to resist the temptation to use questions as weapons when you're angry. Or scared. You have to ignore the people who say, "There's no such thing as a stupid question," blissfully unaware of how important stupid questions are. You have to keep walking toward the questions you're afraid of. Running toward them, even. Even when the shame is tugging at your sleeve, whispering that it's safer to stay quiet.

Nailing Courageous Curiosity isn't like downloading a meditation app. Or journaling sometimes. It's messier. Harder. More painful than anyone is likely to tell you. And to live a Courageously Curious life is to accept that stupid questions will always carry risk.

Asking anyway opens you up. To discomfort. To doubt. To the chance you'll fall flat. But every breakthrough I've seen? Every person who finally got unstuck? They all started the same way, by finally asking that one stupid question.

The cost of moving forward is a
willingness to stumble. *Ask anyway.*

The right stupid question doesn't always just show you the path. Sometimes, it also hands you the bricks to build your own. So when you're ready to ask? I hope you do.

I did.

REALIZING YOU'RE SPRINTING IN THE WRONG DIRECTION HURTS MORE THAN FAILURE.

7

THE DOUBT

I stared at my laptop, trapped in that basement chemistry lab like a mouse in a cage. The question had been scratching the back of my throat for weeks. Until, whether I liked it or not, it tore out of me.

"What the HELL am I even DOING?!"

On the surface, everything seemed stable a year after I decided not to quit the PhD. Emily and I had moved in together. In a new apartment. With better lighting. We'd said, "I love you" for the first time. We'd rescued dogs. We'd tried to build something real. But underneath it all, something was fraying. The future I had been working so hard for felt … fragile.

Professionally, I was still in it. A few days after I chose not to quit, one of the two remaining professors agreed to take me in. It wasn't easy, but within a week, I was running new experiments again. But the new lab was nothing like the old one. Where my first advisor's lab had included towering windows and a third-floor view, this lab was tucked deep in the basement. No distractions. No natural light. Just concrete walls and a silence that rang in my ears.

I sat there, staring at my laptop.

For two and a half years, I'd buried myself in research, chasing data, chasing progress, chasing something. But now, in that quiet, cramped, airless room, the question finally caught up with me: *What comes next?*

Up until that moment, I'd gotten through school on autopilot. I liked chemistry. I liked solving problems. I liked figuring things out down to the dancing molecules. I never stopped to question what it was all building toward. I just assumed—naively—that earning a PhD meant my future would be limitless.

There was a statistic that the grad students around me used to repeat back then: "Only 1% of people ever earn a PhD." We wore it like a badge of honor, proof that we were part of an elite class. But that day, the thought wouldn't stop bugging me: *Has anyone ever verified that?*

Curious, I typed, "Jobs for PhD chemists." The results hit like a gut punch. Oil and gas in remote towns. Pharma, plastics, perfume. None of that felt like me. I kept scrolling. Hoping. And as I scrolled, the sinking feeling sank deeper. The only listings that sparked even a flicker were the ones that involved teaching.

By now, I'd spent years TA'ing, tutoring, mentoring. And it wasn't until I scrolled through that list that it hit me that I didn't just like teaching. I *needed* it. I wasn't in this for the research. I was in it for *them*. The spark in their eyes when it finally *clicks*. Teaching was the part of the PhD I loved the most. Maybe that was it; maybe I should become a tenured university professor. That had to be the path, right? Teaching at any lower level didn't require a PhD. But *this* did. So maybe—just maybe—this was what I had been building toward all along.

I typed in the next search, "How to get a job as a university professor in chemistry." But the numbers were worse than I expected. For every tenure-track job in chemistry, there were seven PhD-holders lined up to take it. I scratched out some numbers in my notebook. Looked once. Then again. But I received the same answer. There was no mistake. About a 5% chance. Maybe 15% if I got lucky. And that was *if* I wanted the job that half my classmates were already chasing. Classmates who were already a year and a half ahead of me.

None of us wanted to work in Oil & Gas. None of us wanted to work in plastics. We were all fighting for the same handful of chairs.

That sinking feeling anchored to the bottom. What exactly had I been racing toward?

I kept scrolling and found an NPR story from 2013 titled, *"Are There Too Many Ph.D.s And Not Enough Jobs?"*

I hesitated, then clicked. The article followed a few of the thousands of PhD holders who couldn't find work. And after years of trying, they were barely scraping by. As lab techs. As bartenders.

Emily had asked me to spend more time together. How many times had I told her, "I have to work late again?" My sister, a medical doctor herself, had warned me too. "You're killing yourself working with those chemicals, you know." But the worst part wasn't what they said. The worst part was knowing, deep down, that they were right.

I was sprinting toward a 95% chance of failure. With every late night. Every missed moment. And for what? How had I not seen it? How had I let it get this far?

"What the HELL am I even DOING?!"

SOMETIMES CLARITY DOESN'T ROAR. SOMETIMES IT JUST SHRUGS AND HANDS YOU A COOKIE.

8

THE ANSWER

I'd asked the question dozens of times before. But this time was the breaking point. "What do you recommend?"

The room was full of graduate students munching on cookies and sandwiches. A few of them rolled their eyes. That stung. I'd been asking this question for months, desperate for clarity. And every time, I got the same thing. Nothing. This time *had* to be different. I needed help.

It felt like a coin flip was about to decide the rest of my life. Academia or industry; those were the only two options for a chemistry PhD. But neither one felt like me. And it mattered now. This wasn't just about me anymore. Emily was patient, but I wasn't going to drag her into a future I didn't believe in. Yet neither path looked as clear to me as it seemed to look for everyone around me.

I hunted for the answer everywhere. I asked everyone I could, which career should I aim for. But nobody could answer. Not really. And when they fumbled, I'd follow up with, "Well ... what do you want to do?"

Some said academia. Some said industry. Almost none of them were confused about it. They knew where they were going. It was obvious.

I didn't, and that was obvious too.

Most of the other students in the chemistry department had chemist parents. Mentors. People who had already guided them. My dad was a mechanic. My mom worked in insurance and at a grocery store. That had never seemed important until I realized I might've missed out on some secret roadmap. One that everyone else had been handed years ago.

But there was one thing I knew for sure: No matter which path I chose, the road ahead would be steep. If I stayed in academia, the ghost of my former advisor would haunt me forever. And if I jumped into industry, I'd have to pivot into an entirely different world. A world filled with people who hadn't wasted years grinding through a chemistry PhD.

Regardless, I wasn't quitting the PhD. Not after everything I'd been through. My new advisor had taken me in when no one else would. He was kind. Patient. He didn't ask for much. But I owed him, and the least I could do was finish what I'd started.

I'd grown tired of asking the same question—industry or academia— and getting nowhere. But today felt different. We had a guest professor visiting.

Every semester, the department flew one in for a part networking opportunity, part show-and-tell. The department pretended it was fair; free lunch, open questions. But we all knew the real game. A few students would lob hyper-specific questions, hoping to impress after spending weeks memorizing every piece of that professor's research. While the rest of us? We enjoyed a lunch and watched.

But this day ... something broke. Maybe the star student was sick. Maybe nobody cared enough. Either way, the room sat in awkward silence. Nobody asked anything. And every little sound echoed, from someone clearing their throat to opening a candy wrapper. So, I raised my hand.

"How did you end up getting a job at one of the top Ivy League schools? That's a pretty big deal, right?"

The guest smiled. "Funny thing is, they actually rejected me the first time."

I blinked. "What?"

"Yeah. I pitched my research idea to them in the early 2000s, and they told me it wouldn't work. So, I took a job at a smaller school that gave me a shot, and then I published a few papers. It worked. Then the Ivy came calling." He leaned back, grinning. "Felt nice to flip the script."

A hand went up on the far side of the room. The guest didn't see it. And I kept going.

"Whoa. I mean, as impressive as that is, it's also kind of unsurprising. The work you've done is phenomenal. Did you always know you wanted to be a professor and chase this research project?"

He thought about it. "I always knew I wanted to be a professor, yes. But the project? That came later from an idea I had during my graduate work."

Out of the corner of my eye, I saw the raised hand go down.

I nodded eagerly, and—sensing the window was still wide open—decided to risk it. "I'm personally struggling with that myself," I said. "I don't know whether I want to go into academia or industry. What do you recommend?"

He didn't miss a beat. "People only become professors because it's important to them to see their name on papers. To prove to the world they're smart. Myself included. Nothing else really mattered when I made the decision, and it doesn't for most professors either."

I stared at him. He said it so casually. By this point, nobody else in the room existed anymore as I pushed back. "That can't be true for everyone. What about the ones who love teaching?" I was thinking about my new advisor. It felt like a betrayal to imagine him chasing ego instead of ideas.

The guest shrugged. "Doesn't matter. If we cared more about the research than the recognition, we'd be in industry making a lot more money. But we don't. We want our name in journals. Next to the discovery."

And just like that, everything made sense.

"Well," I said flatly, "looking smart is the farthest thing from my mind."

He replied just as flat. "Then go into industry. You'll make more money. And if you love teaching, you'll find plenty of mentorship opportunities there too." He casually took another bite of his cookie.

After all the spinning, all the searching, all the nights I'd spent convincing myself that this choice would shape the rest of my life, I didn't expect the answer to come with a cookie.

It felt lopsided. Like I'd been dragging a piano up a mountain, only to realize I could've just walked around it. No grand philosophy. No deeper wisdom. Just a brutally simple truth.

I sat with it for a few minutes while the guest answered a couple more questions. But then someone said the lunch was done, and I couldn't get up fast enough.

I had the answer now. I had to *move*.

SOMETIMES THE BRAVEST THING YOU CAN DO IS GET UP AND RUN.

9

THE CHOICE

What is WRONG with me? The thought hit like a hammer against the inside of my skull.

I sat frozen in the break room, fists curled into my knees, on the verge of tears. My phone had fallen to the floor. It was still open to the last thing I'd googled: *How to do well on a phone interview.*

I'd walked out of the lunch with that guest professor with conviction for the first time in months. I had a real answer. A real path forward. Maybe even a way out. I'd almost sprinted to the basement to get my laptop to scour blogs and Reddit for advice. Anything about breaking out of science into something else. I'd read every article I could find about "nontraditional careers for PhD chemists." I'd overhauled my resume. Got PhotoShop and learned how to use it. Designed a business card from scratch, something that looked professional that I could hand over like it mattered. I'd even sent it with my resume. Everywhere. Anywhere. I'd lost count within the first week.

I didn't just want out—I *needed* out. I'd looked up the schedule for the upcoming career fair. Just two weeks away. So I'd started making a list of companies worth visiting, tables worth approaching; anything else that might get me out. I'd only gotten halfway down the list when the email landed in my inbox:

NASA - Callback request for an interview.

I'd stared at the screen, frozen. That was it. My way out. One of my desperate applications had actually gotten a response. Was this for the internship? Yes. Helping test a piece of chemical analysis equipment for the Mars Rover Perseverance.

I'd stopped everything. I'd read everything I could about NASA. The mission. The rover. Two rovers? I'd taught myself how to code in Python and downloaded AutoCAD, having no clue what it was but forcing myself through it anyway. I'd delayed the interview as long as I could, trying to cram more skills into my head. I'd convinced myself I was destined to become an astronaut, and that this was just the first step.

I'd dreamed of all the ways I could leave a lasting impact on the human race. So I dove in, headfirst, excited to absolutely *nail* this and so focused on getting it *perfect*.

But the day finally came. And I'd forgotten to find a quiet place to take the call. I was in the lab. It was loud. So I ran into the nearby stairwell minutes before and stood there alone, waiting.

Then my phone rang, and I scrambled to accept the call.

"Hi, is this Travis?"

I'd blurted out—way too loud—"Yes, hi!"

A pause. Then, *"Okay, great. We've got you on speaker, and the hiring panel is here. Are you ready to get started?"*

Terror sank like a stone in my gut. With a shaking voice, I'd barely gotten out, "Yes."

Each person on the panel had introduced themselves. A few had asked questions about my PhD research. I could tell they were trying to help me relax. And it worked. By the time the question I'd been dreading finally came, I'd felt ready.

"Tell us about being a mechanic. What kind of hands-on experience do you have from that?"

I'd delivered it exactly the way I'd rehearsed. The way I told myself they'd want to hear it. "Well, I'm glad you asked. That's a *great* question. I really loved the fully immersive, multi-dimensional problem solving of fixing cars. I worked in New England, where everything rusts. So no job was ever easy. I had to think two steps ahead—not just take the bolt off, but figure out how to do it without snapping it. I think that kind of cautious thinking would carry over really well into a role at NASA."

I was sure I'd nailed it. But I was only answered by silence at first. Until another voice said, *"Oh, okay. Cool. So, what kind of stuff did you do?"*

Wait, what? That wasn't how it was supposed to go. They were supposed to say, *"That's exactly the kind of person we need."* That's how it had gone in my head when I'd been practicing.

Panic had crawled into my throat. "What do you mean?"

They'd started to respond, but right when they did, someone had opened the stairwell door. They'd seen me on the phone and excitedly whispered, "When's your NASA interview?"

I'd waved them off, panicked, and by the time they left, the person at NASA had finished talking. And I'd missed whatever they'd said.

Terror sank in deeper. "Well, my dad worked on all kinds of cars, you know?" I'd pressed on. "So I got to face the same problems on different models. Made it harder, you know? I loved that kind of difficulty. I'm hoping to find that same challenge in this internship."

More silence followed. For even longer than the first time.

"Um. Okay. I see. Well, thank you for taking the time. Do you have any questions for us?"

I didn't. We said goodbye. And for a moment, when I finally hung up, I could breathe again. I was safe. Until I knew that I'd blown it. Not because I wasn't qualified. Not because I didn't know the answers. I'd blown it because I was too scared to let them see who I really was. Someone who grew up wrenching on cars. Spilling oil all over myself and dropping the occasional tire on my foot.

I still carried too much shame about that version of me.

I'd wandered to the graduate student break room and collapsed into a chair. A part of me thought, *Maybe they'll cut me a break. Maybe it's not too late.* So, I pulled out my phone and searched, "How to do well on a phone interview."

The first bullet hit like a brick: *Always respond to questions in as few words as possible—and authentically. Just answer the question.*

What's wrong with me? I'd had a perfect opportunity drop into my lap, and I'd thrown it away. *What's wrong with me?* Why did I DO that? *How could I do something so stupid?* Why the hell had I taken that call in a stairwell? *Why do I always do this?*

I sat there, drowning in it until a friend walked in. Another student. She slowed when she saw me, tears now streaking down my face.

She didn't ask about the interview. Everyone already knew. Someone saw. Or heard. Instead, she just asked, "Are you okay?"

All I could do was shake my head. I couldn't talk. I stared down at my hands. Maybe this was it. Maybe I wasn't cut out for this. Maybe I should just quit.

Then she said the words that changed *everything*. "Well, hey, did you hear? Tesla's here on campus. And they're going to be at the career fair tomorrow. They're doing a big presentation tonight. You should go. I was thinking of you when I heard about it. Didn't you work on cars before?"

A tiny spark flickered, but I tried to kill it. I was sick of hope.

"They're over at the math and science building," she continued. "I think their talk starts at seven?"

I hesitated. It felt safe to sit there. Safe to stay broken. I didn't want to hope again. Not so soon. Not after I'd just been burned so hard. But I couldn't help myself. I looked at my watch. *6:45.* So I ran. I ran as fast as I could, forgetting my phone on the floor of the break room. And as I ran, I laughed at myself.

The cool wind wiped the tears from my cheeks.

REDEMPTION IS EARNED BY STAYING TRUE TO YOURSELF WHEN IT'S HARDEST TO.

10

THE STAND

I stood at the front of the line of students to talk to Tesla. The recruiter looked right past me. He waved at the person behind me, clearly motioning for them to step forward instead.

My heart raced. My shirt stuck to my back. I walked up anyway.

It took me ten minutes to reach Tesla's presentation that night. And by the time I got there—6:55 sharp—the room was packed. I was out of breath, and it was standing room only. Hundreds of students jammed wall-to-wall, every seat was filled.

Three people from Tesla each took a turn to speak. The first guy was a mechanic. He loved working on cars because he'd been doing it his whole life, and he wanted an intern who was the same way. I smiled without meaning to, thinking about my dad. I'd wrenched on more cars with him than I could count.

The second speaker had studied sustainability in college. She talked about how important it was to her that she worked somewhere that made a real impact on the planet. I perked up. Sustainability and Green Chemistry is what I was studying now after switching advisors.

The third speaker stood up. He had a PhD in Polymer Chemistry from MIT. And he needed an intern who understood chemistry. And cars. Someone who could start in Palo Alto, then move to the Gigafactory in Reno.

My jaw dropped. The NASA internship evaporated from my mind. This was it. *This* was my shot. And this time, I could physically reach out and touch it.

But I couldn't. The second the presentation ended, a stampede started. More than a hundred engineering students surged forward, forming a massive line. I glanced at it, snaking across the room and packed tight, swarming around the presenters.

I clenched my jaw. I should wait. I should get in line. This was my shot.

But … I had to grade fifty lab reports. They were waiting for me at home. And if I stayed in the line, I'd be up all night. On the other hand, if I left, I might never get another chance. The weight of the decision crushed my chest.

I turned and walked away, deciding to catch Tesla at the career fair the next day instead.

It was a long night. I graded all fifty lab reports, reworked my business cards to highlight my mechanic background and printed a new stack, polished my resume, and ironed my suit. I finally made it to bed by 2:00 A.M.

The next day was the busiest day of the week. I had class until 10:30

A.M, followed by back-to-back teaching labs from 11:00 A.M. to 5:00 P.M. But the career fair was only open from 10:00 A.M. to 2:00 P.M. And located across campus. Of course.

I had exactly thirty minutes to sprint across campus and drop off my resume, then race back to prep my lab. Sure, I could've asked someone to cover for me. But there was a student I wanted to talk with about last week's lab. Someone who mattered. Because they needed help. So I never even considered it.

Everything was going smoothly—until I got to the career fair. And saw the line. Hundreds of engineering students, snaking around the fair and down the hallway. Even out of the building.

I stopped at the end and asked the kid in front of me how long the wait was.

He glanced down at my suit and smirked. "Word is, two hours."

Two hours?! I had twenty minutes left before I had to be teaching lab. And skipping the lab wasn't an option. Not even a thought.

I hesitated. I could either hand in the resume in five minutes. Or not hand it in at all.

My legs decided before my mind could.

My heart pounded as I strolled past that kid. And the next. I kept walking. I strode—maybe too briskly—until I was at the front of the line. The kid at the front barely had time to react before I blurted out, "I have to teach a lab in five minutes. Do you mind if I just drop this off?"

He shook his head, clearly annoyed.

The Tesla recruiter saw me do it. He gave me a look. You know the look. The 'who do you think you are?' look. The 'get in line like everyone else' look. He finished with the current student, then waved for the *kid behind me* to come up. He made it clear; I wasn't welcome.

For a second, I stood there, frozen, waiting for him to say something. To acknowledge me. To prove I hadn't made a mistake. But he didn't. And after another second, the certainty drained out of me.

But I walked forward anyway. Before I even reached the table, I extended my resume, business card attached.

"Listen," I said, trying not to shake. "I don't have time to stand in line. I have to go teach a lab right now. But I'm the intern you're looking for. I promise you. I need this. And you need me."

He didn't say a word. He just looked at the resume, frowning. Then tossed it into a pile and waved the next kid forward. Again. That was it.

I stood there for a second longer, hoping he'd say something. Anything. But he didn't. So I turned and walked away. Past every kid who stared daggers into me. My ears burned. My chest pounded. And all the frantic work of the past day hit me like a freight train.

The NASA call. The devastation. The crying. The run toward grace. The resume. The business cards. Cutting the line—it had all been a good distraction. But now the distraction was gone. And all that was left as I raced to teach the lab was shame.

The look on that Tesla recruiter's face was burned into my memory. Who did I think I was? In less than twenty-four hours, I'd embarrassed myself in front of NASA *and* Tesla. What the hell was wrong with me?

Had I learned nothing? Was I just repeating the same mistakes I made a year ago? Arrogance? Overconfidence? Charging into something unprepared? Had I come this far only to fall right back?

Emily was really kind to me that night. We settled in to watch a movie, armed with popcorn and ice cream.

Then it happened. At 6:37 P.M., my phone rang. And the caller ID displayed a Massachusetts area code. My pulse spiked, and I almost didn't pick up.

"… Hello?"

"Hey, I'm calling from Tesla Motors. Are you the kid who cut the whole line? What—you think you're special or something?"

I froze. *No f*cking way.*

I didn't overthink it. I just answered. Honestly. Simply. The way I should have answered all along, even with my heart trying to beat out of my chest. And three weeks, two more interviews, and a whole lot of fear later, I had it locked in.

I was going to Tesla.

CLEANING UP THE MESS MIGHT HURT, BUT MAKING IT IS EXHILARATING.

11

THE MESS

You hand your toddler a cup of milk. Their grip is loose. They're wobbly. You brace for the inevitable spill, worried. But if you never let them try, if you always keep the cup out of reach, you rob them of the chance to grow.

Raising kids is messy. If you've raised children, you don't need me to explain. If you haven't, just imagine the first time you hand a kid toilet paper and say, "You can wipe all on your own!"

Parenting is messy. Growth comes with mistakes. And courageous curiosity is no different.

Asking a courageous question invites criticism. Sometimes from people too scared to ask themselves. Sometimes from people who don't understand why it takes courage to ask at all. But it's in making the mess—spilling the milk—that we learn.

Those who say, "There's no such thing as a stupid question," mean well. But they're like the parent who snatches the cup back, annoyed you might drop it. Whether they realize it or not, they're trying to protect us from stumbling and fumbling. But stumbling and fumbling through our shame is exactly how we grow.

Courageous curiosity without
stumbling and fumbling isn't
courageous at all.

The mess and frustration you feel when asking stupid questions pretty much always comes back to shame. And it shows up in two ways:

- The kind you build inside your own head (*Fabricated Shame*)
- The kind others throw at you (*Applied Shame*)

Fabricated shame is fear you created in your own head. Past mistakes. Old scars. Stories you've come to believe about yourself. No one says them out loud. You do that part on your own.

Applied shame comes from the outside. The comment. The eye roll. The silence you didn't expect. The look that says, "You should have known better." Shame is almost always at the root of the frustration you feel when asking stupid questions.

Sometimes it's *Fabricated*. Sometimes *Applied*. Sometimes both. But when it hits you, you know. That was a stupid question. And that's the whole point. Then you can start to figure out what that question was. And why you needed to ask it out loud. Or still do. You won't always spot it right away. But once you start paying attention, you'll see it everywhere. The questions holding people back. The questions stopping others. The ones stopping you.

> The shame thrown at your question
> is either yours or theirs. Know the
> difference and keep moving.

Let's look at the stories I told. Let's find out what was what:

- When I found out my career was going nowhere, the weight of my mistake crushed me. That was fabricated shame.

- When I asked the guest professor for a recommendation, the rolling eyes burned into me. That was applied shame.

- When I bombed my NASA interview, I spiraled into self-loathing. That was fabricated shame *before*, *during*, and *after* asking the stupid question.

- When I cut the Tesla line, my heart pounded in terror of both success and failure. That shame was fabricated and applied *before*, *during*, and *after* asking the stupid question. And this memory is seared into my brain because of *how much it hurt*.

But how do we figure out where the *fabricated* shame comes from? And what do we do about it?

There are a million ways to work through this kind of shame. Books. Podcasts. Therapy. Conversations with people who care. I'm not here to tell you *how* to do it. But I am here to tell you that it's your job. You have to pick up the cup of milk. You have to be the one to spill it. And yeah, you have to clean up the mess. If you don't? You'll stay stuck.

Living courageously curious means putting yourself in the path of your own fabricated shame with intention. And cleaning up the mess after you stumble through it. Not *despite* your fear of it. But *because* of it. It's the only way to get through it. And if you don't put in the work to understand what your fabricated shame is, you won't be able to find it.

> Put in the work to find your fabricated
> shame so you can sprint into it.

Applied shame is trickier, because it hits you out of nowhere. You can't predict when someone's going to make fun of your question. Or fire off a comment that makes you shrink inside. Or roll their eyes. Or laugh at you instead of with you. You can't predict when someone will throw applied shame at you. Sometimes it's intentional. Sometimes it's not. And most of the time, it doesn't even *look* like shame at first glance. That's why it can be so tricky to spot.

> You don't want to dodge applied
> shame; you want to recognize it.
> So sharpen your radar.

It's silly, but it works. Ask something small and silly. Ask questions that even you think *should* get a little criticism. Real questions, but questions that still feel silly and small. Ask, then sit back. Tiptoe your way into courageous curiosity. Watch and see how others respond. You won't feel crushed by the response, but you'll feel *something*. And that's a start. And, after doing that enough, you'll start to recognize the feeling when it hits you in the wild, making you that much more prepared and able to respond.

Going back to our toddler with milk: start with dry cereal first. Use a plastic bowl. Let some of the cereal miss their mouth. It's messy but not catastrophic. And that's the point. You won't walk away covered in milk. They won't either. And as the messes get bigger, you'll get a little better at not flinching.

Eventually that toddler will be able to handle spaghetti with red sauce. Ask tiny, low-risk stupid questions. Like, "Wait, what's a Roth IRA?" at a finance workshop. Or, "What does that acronym mean?" in a meeting full of veterans. You'll feel the shame ripple through you, but you'll survive. And you'll learn who's safe to ask.

Let the reaction of others guide your own. And build your tolerance so that when it really matters, you won't blink.

> Tiptoe into applied shame consistently
> with low-risk stupid questions.

It sounds simple, but that doesn't necessarily make it easy. When my former advisor simply recommended I save my tears for my girlfriend instead? That was like throwing a basketball on the kitchen table. And it was an invitation for the mess that followed.

The alternative is to put in the work. Aim for a courageously curious life. Get to know your fabricated shame so you can run into it with intention. Get to know how applied shame feels by tiptoeing into it enough times. Eventually, you'll start to feel almost comfortable in it. And at some point, it'll become quite exhilarating to ask stupid questions.

If you're anything like me, you'll start to rush into asking them. You'll look for chances to. Kind of like I did after my crisis. But if you get to this point, I have another word of caution for you.

You're still the toddler with a glass of milk. Don't throw milk all over those around you. They deserve better. Save the mess for yourself. It's yours, not theirs. And their mess is theirs. Let them keep it.

> Don't give those around you the task of
> asking your stupid questions for you.

Just like you have to carry your own cup of milk, so do they.

If someone can't answer your stupid question for you, move on. Don't push them. And don't ask what their stupid questions are so you can find the answers for them. Don't do the work *for* someone else.

If a friend tells you a question they're scared to ask, don't rush to ask it *for* them. Even if you're trying to help. Even if it seems kind. You don't know their full story. You don't know what they've wrestled with, or what they'll gain by asking it themselves. When you step in too soon, you steal their shot.

It's like handing that cup of milk to the toddler, keeping your hands wrapped around theirs the whole time, and celebrating when nothing spills. They didn't learn. You didn't really help.

> Ask questions because *you* need the answer. No other reason. And only ask stupid questions out of an earnest desire to find answers *for yourself*.

Every stupid question I've asked has had one thing in common: they've all came from *me*. My curiosity. My shame. My fear. And yours will, too.

If you're scared to ask, that's your sign. If your chest tightens, if your stomach drops, that's your signal that you're onto something. That's your fabricated shame trying to hold you back. And if people react with side-eyes or snickers? That's the applied shame. Let it roll off and keep going. Because the only way through shame is through it. And the only way to get better at asking is by asking.

Ask a lot of questions. Ask messily. Ask often. And the next time you have a question burning in your gut, don't hesitate. Ask it. Even when you're riding high. Even when you feel like you're on top of the world.

Like I was. As a wide-eyed intern about to start at Tesla. You'd think I was on top of the world. And I was—for about five minutes. But courageous curiosity doesn't end when the doors finally open. That's when it gets real.

And yes, it knocked me flat.

WHEN THE SMALLEST MOMENT MAKES YOU QUESTION THE BIGGEST ONES.

12

THE FREEZE

The air in the small conference room felt heavy. Someone shifted in their seat. The low hum of conversations bled through the walls. My boss looked over, eyebrows raised. The three other people who'd just introduced themselves looked confused.

My throat closed tight. I froze. *What do I say?*

My first two weeks at Tesla were chaos. But it was a comfortable chaos. Here, knowledge flowed freely. There was no bickering about it. The structure was simple: Disagree with your boss? Tell their boss. Still stuck? Email Elon. Every aspect of working there imbued a demand for confidence and speed. Even I—the intern—was told the same. It was the complete opposite of academia's stiff hierarchy. And the only rule was to help whoever needed help, no questions asked. Outside of that? I never knew what was coming next.

Every bumper-to-bumper commute, I'd wonder, *What's today's curveball?*

One surprise that crept up slowly was the realization that nobody there had advanced degrees. In academia, having a PhD was like having a golden ticket. Without it, you were just another name on the list. But at Tesla? Almost no one had a PhD. Because they didn't need one. Especially my boss. He was Sharp. Rugged. Yet, somehow, he had no edges. He never mentioned his doctorate, so if you didn't already know about it, you never would. He just did the work. And invited everyone to do it with him. And that alone was the biggest gift he gave me. He made me feel ... normal.

For the first time, I started to think that maybe my PhD didn't have to define me. It didn't have to be the bookmark. It could be in the appendix while I was busy living. And it felt amazing. I felt unstoppable.

I started asking questions, chasing answers, and keeping up with the engineers years ahead of me. I didn't feel like an intern. I felt like I belonged. Every day felt like a first. And today's first? A big one—my first supplier chat. My first time representing Tesla to an outsider.

I was pumped. Couldn't wait to meet new people and solve new problems. And as a bonus, the supplier team all had PhDs. So I was excited to see more of that blunt, ego-free culture my boss had normalized for me. By now, I'd totally bought into it. Which is exactly why I was so shocked by what came next.

I walked into the room expecting another fast, no-frills Tesla meeting. But something felt ... off. Three men in suits sat at the table. For the first time since starting my internship, I felt underdressed. It felt like being back in the chemistry department, where professors wore suits when they wanted to *show off*. But I tried to shake it off. *This is Tesla*, I reminded myself. *Tesla's different.*

I opened my laptop and started typing notes. I'd just gotten through the word *Attendees* when my boss burst in. He clapped his hands and said, "Alright! Should we do some introductions?" without even sitting down.

They jumped right in. I kept typing. But within seconds, my stomach dropped. Every name came with a brand. Stanford. Harvard. Princeton. MIT. And then it was my turn.

Followed by silence. Way too much silence. My mind raced. *Is this normal? Why are they all listing their schools? Did I miss something?* Four seconds. Five. Six. Then it hit me: every single person in the room had an Ivy League degree. Except me. And in those seconds, I fell from the top of the world to the bottom.

I shrank inside. Embarrassed. I started shaking, and my chest tightened. *What do I say?* But I had no time left to think. And I knew whatever came out would sound ... off. Would make it obvious that I wasn't a part of their club. So I just decided to be me.

"Hi, everyone. I'm Travis. I'm a graduate student at the University of Nevada, Reno. I'm interning for him." I motioned weakly toward my boss, my face burning and my hands shaking. I quickly tucked them under the table. And all I could think was, *Why did I say it like that? Why didn't I just say 'Travis Cournoyer, UNR,' like everyone else?*.

The meeting moved on. I made it through. But when it was over, I left feeling tiny. Unworthy. I sat at my desk after the meeting, staring at my screen, but my mind wasn't on my work. It was stuck circling that moment. That feeling. The freeze. And as I sat there, a new question started to dawn on me.

Why had I been so surprised when Tesla called me in the first place? Was it really just the shame of how I'd handed in my resume? Or was it something deeper? Something darker? Maybe I didn't believe I *deserved* to be there. Maybe I'd just gotten lucky. Got away with something. I'd convinced myself that the NASA thing proved I wasn't good enough. And when Tesla called anyway? It rattled my whole story. But there, in that tiny conference room, it felt like the universe had snapped the story back in place.

See? It whispered. *You don't belong here. You never did.*

And I believed it. Every word. That's why my voice had frozen. That's why my hands had shaken. That's why I felt small. But that feeling of smallness wasn't proof I didn't belong. Maybe it was something else pointing me somewhere I didn't want to look.

I had a choice to make. I could stop. I could give up. I could choose to stay small. Or I could get up. Keep going. And *grow*.

WHEN YOUR
BODY MOVES
FASTER THAN
YOUR MIND
AND YOUR
COURAGE
HAS TO
CATCH UP.

13

THE TERROR

"Can you help me take care of it?" I asked, breathless.

Jeff didn't even look up. "You're not serious."

I was. Dead serious. And when he looked at me that way, the terror crumbled into something worse: shame.

Most of my internship was spent moving. Always moving.

I started in the chemistry lab, deep in the basement prepping glue samples, boxing them, then hauling everything upstairs to the prototype shop. There were two ways to get there. The long way by taking the elevator, circling the building, and heading down a staircase. Or the short way, which cut through the outdoor atrium and straight up the stairs. I always took the shortcut. The lab and the shop were far apart, and I spent over an hour a day just walking back and forth between them. Through that atrium, over and over again.

The chemistry lab had been packed the morning I asked this question, so I set up my glue samples outside in the atrium. That's where all the messy work happened, stuff too risky for the sensitive equipment inside. And like any messy area, junk had started to pile up. A couple of nitrogen tanks waiting for the next AirGas pickup. Random hand-tools left on random benches and tables. Pallets of barrels with who-knows-what. You get the picture. But growing up as a mechanic, I always tried to leave my workspace cleaner than I found it. So, even though I was rushing, I made a mental checklist of what I'd tidy up later: The diamond saw, wet from a fresh cut; I'd wipe it down. A black glove or something on the floor; I'd pick it up. Some dirty glassware in a box; I'd bring it inside and scrub it all down. I stashed the list in my head, packed up my box, and headed upstairs.

I barely set the box down in the prototype shop when I froze. I'd forgot my notebook in the atrium again. Damn. I rushed back down to the atrium to grab it. But when my hand hit the notebook, I froze, because something felt off. I ran back through my mental checklist. Nothing should've changed. Nobody had come in. So what was it? The diamond saw? Same. The glassware? Untouched. But something still felt off. And I couldn't figure out what.

I walked over to and grabbed a beaker and checked how grimy it was. Filthy. I turned it over in my hands and glanced down, expecting to see that glove. But it wasn't there. I scanned the floor, confused. The glove was somewhere else—and it was moving. Toward me.

My brain scrambled to catch up. Gloves don't move. Then I saw the legs. Way too many legs. And hair. It wasn't a glove.

My brain lagged behind my body. The beaker shattered on the floor, and I ran. Sprinted inside. Yanked the door shut. Braced it with both arms. My heart pounded so hard, I couldn't breathe. Still, I ran to the nearest person.

Jeff operated the Scanning Electron Microscope. He was typically laid-back and cool under pressure. Nothing shook him. Perfect.

I darted over to him. "Jeff, there's a tarantula in the atrium. Can you please help me take care of it?"

He didn't even flinch. "You're not serious." After a moment's pause, he added, "There's *no way* you're being serious right now. I've worked here for years, and I've never seen a single spider in that atrium. Let alone a tarantula."

"I have arachnophobia," I blurted. "It was a tarantula." I swallowed hard before mumbling, "And ... yeah. Childhood trauma with spiders. Long story."

Why did I say that? What was I trying to prove? What was I trying to avoid?

Jeff sighed. And finally stood up. I watched him disappear toward the atrium, my heart still racing.

Five minutes later, he wandered back in, calm as ever, like he'd just gone to grab a coffee. Jeff sat down again and adjusted the microscope. He got back to work just like that. With no update. Not even a glance in my direction.

I stood there, still frozen. "So ... what happened?"

He blinked like had to mentally hit rewind. "Oh, the spider? It was a California Tarantula. Totally harmless. I scooped it up and let it go in the woods."

I exhaled. Finally. It was done. Okay.

Jeff stretched, his behavior as if we just wrapped up a casual chat. "Oh, there's some broken glass on the floor out there. Looks like somebody dropped a beaker. Be careful." A faint smirk tugged at his lips. Maybe he knew.

"Thanks," I deadpanned.

He just smiled and went back to work.

I stood there, thinking. I could have left it. I could have reasoned my way into ignoring it. Pretended it wasn't my problem. Avoided that atrium forever. But I grabbed a broom before I fully understood why. And as I stepped up to the door, my hands kept shaking and my heart continued racing. I stood there a second longer until it hit me.

I'd already spent so much of this internship walking. Back and forth. From room to room. Wasting time covering the same ground again and again. But now, it was something different. A new kind of walk. Not just moving for the sake of moving but stepping toward something I was actually afraid of. Something that might actually change me. All that aimless motion? It kept me busy. But it didn't get me anywhere. This step would.

So, I gripped the broom more tightly. Tears beaded along my lashes, my jaw fully clenched. I took a breath. And walked back out into the atrium. Still shaking. Still scared.

WHEN PAIN, PRIDE, AND PRIVILEGE COLLIDE IN THE SAME HALLWAY.

14

THE SWEAT

My back ached. Sweat dripped into my eyes. The doors balanced on my shoulders felt twice as heavy as they had that morning. Still, I kept moving. There was no solution in sight, but stopping wasn't an option.

The project didn't care that I was exhausted. It wasn't slowing down. And neither could I.

Then, right as my legs started screaming the loudest, someone walked toward a golf cart. My savior. Finally.

I called out, "Hey, can I hitch a ride?"

His whole posture changed. I was too scared to be confused. I just braced for whatever was about to happen.

I'd spent a few weeks of my Tesla internship at the production plant in Fremont, which was nothing like headquarters. HQ was the future, teams working on concepts one, two, ten models ahead of what was on the production line. While the plant was the now. The grit. Actual cars. The scramble. Live assembly. Constant motion. Stepping from headquarters into the plant felt like stepping back in time. And it was pure chaos.

But not that comfortable chaos.

Where HQ had a rhythm, a bit of an ebb and flow, the plant was relentless. It HAD to be. I'd been sent over to help solve a stubborn problem on the falcon wing doors for the Model X. A bracket needed to be glued in place. But every time they glued it, the glue shrank, leaving visible dimples on the door. It looked terrible, and my job was to fix it. And there was no going back to HQ until I did.

The task was simple enough on paper. Get the glue to hold the bracket in place without causing damage to the door. But when I asked how I could check if the dimples were too deep, the technician let out a deep laugh.

"Oh, you don't." He clapped me on the back. "You glue it, get the door painted, and take it to the design studio. They'll put it under a microscope and tell you if you messed up." He smirked. "If they can't find the dimples, you win." He seemed way too happy to give me this task.

I started to worry. "How many times have you tried this?"

He waved me off, already turning to leave. It was obvious he needed a break. "You have ten doors left. That's it. Figure it out." As he hit the doorway, he paused and added, "Oh, and don't forget they have to go through E-coat before paint."

The door swung shut behind him.

I pulled out my notebook and made a priority list.

- Figure out what E-coat is (and where it happens)

- Find the paint shop

- Find the design studio

- Trial 1: Half the UV light for curing

Then got to work.

The first door was an adventure. I glued on a few brackets in random spots, each with a slightly different tweak to the curing process, and hoisted the thing up. Then I wandered aimlessly around the plant, asking anyone I passed, "Where's E-coat?" When I eventually found it, I dropped the door in the queue and asked the tech how long it would take.

"About forty-five minutes," he said.

Perfect.

I grabbed lunch, then came back to track down the paint shop the same way. It was located in another building, tucked behind the plant. So I carried the door over and added it to their rack. When they asked what color, I reasoned black would be best.

"We'll spray it in ten minutes, but it needs twenty to dry," the tech said.

So I waited, then lugged the door all the way across the plant to the design studio, less than one hundred feet from the room where I'd glued the brackets in the first place. Of course. I staggered in, out of breath, arms shaking. Only to realize just how heavy that door was.

I placed it gently onto the designer's desk, trying to sound upbeat. "Do you think you can find the dimples?"

She smiled. She was calm. She gently put down her book and lowered her glasses. With a light raised, she delicately picked up her defect-marking pen and, with surgical precision, circled every single dimple for every single bracket I'd glued. Then she looked up at me, eyes bright. "Did I get them all?"

My head dropped. "Yeah."

Her eyes softened. A silent apology. She knew I'd be back.

I managed two doors that day. Three more the next. By day four, I ran out of doors, but I still wasn't anywhere near a solution. Every single door? All the dimples were found.

When I told my boss I needed more doors, he didn't even blink. "I know where we can scavenge more. Come on." He decided to join me that day, likely frustrated I'd been pulled away from my main project for so long.

We marched to a corner of the plant I didn't know existed and dug through a giant scrap pile until we found and hauled back ten more doors on a rickety cart.

By day eight, I was wrecked. My back and neck screamed. My shoulders throbbed. I had blisters on both feet. I took each trip two doors at a time by now. I reasoned it would end the project faster, but it was misery. My body was ready to quit. And the endless back-and-forth had become torture. Then, I spotted him.

Someone cutting straight for the golf carts.

I'd passed those carts a hundred times, always wondering who had the keys, but nobody ever seemed to know. Now, though, I was sure. He had them. And this was my shot. My saving grace. Buoyed by that we-all-help-each-other vibe Tesla had drilled into me, I felt bold. Like redemption was finally mine.

So I shouted, "Hey, can I hitch a ride?"

His head snapped around. His jaw clenched, eyes narrowed. He locked eyes with me, and I swear I could feel the fury radiating off him as he stormed toward me. Each step louder, faster. I braced myself, fully expecting to get fired on the spot.

Then—thank God—my boss appeared out of nowhere. He hustled over, stepped between us, and said, "Hey, he's just an intern. He doesn't know any better."

The guy rolled his eyes, huffed, and stormed back to his cart. He climbed in, turned the key ... and nothing. He'd forgotten to charge it. He spiked the keys into the ground and let out a yell of pure frustration before stomping off.

My boss turned to me and sighed. "Golf carts? Those are for the *most important people* at the plant. Even I can't use one. Never ask again." And just like that, he was gone again.

I stood there, catching my breath, with the doors biting into my shoulders. I adjusted my grip and looked down at the long, familiar path ahead. And I took another step, wincing at the pain. I was too hurt and tired to take anything away from it then. But as I sat in the paint shop waiting for the doors an hour later, a question materialized that I couldn't ignore.

Why was being an intern relevant? Why did he say that, of all things? And why did it work? I turned that question in my head for years. Trying to make sense of it.

Regardless, a few days later, the moment came. I placed a door on that desk in that design studio, meeting her kind eyes again. After her inspection, she asked if she'd found all the brackets.

I stood tall and confidently as I said, "No. Not this time." It was my turn to watch while she sat with the discomfort. Worried that we might *actually* glue this bracket to the door. She finally started to believe that we might. But I'd figured out how to solve my part, so it wasn't my problem anymore. Now, it was her problem to *keep* it solved.

Every time I see a Model X out in the wild, even now, I still check those Falcon wing doors. Just to be sure.

Funny thing, though, solving that problem wasn't the part that stuck with me. It was that question. The one I couldn't let go of. Why was being an intern the thing that saved me? And what did that really mean?

WHEN
CONFIDENCE
WALKS YOU
IN AND
HUMILITY
GETS YOU
OUT ALIVE.

15

THE ARROGANCE

I took a confident breath. It was September 2016, and I stood before a room full of engineers in Los Angeles. Engineers I'd met for the first time twenty minutes earlier. "Any questions?" I asked, scanning the room, ready for a wave of rapid-fire challenges.

But all I received was silence.

My stomach dropped. There were furrowed brows. And some tapping fingers. This wasn't grad school. It wasn't even Tesla. I'd made a mistake. A big one.

My Tesla internship had stretched into its 15th month before my boss pulled me aside to talk about where I'd be going next. A hiring freeze was about to come down the pipeline, and my internship was going to end. So, I started applying for internships for the next summer. Just internships. I was playing the long game: finish my PhD, line up another internship, and hopefully end up in a full-time job at Tesla by fall 2017. At least, that was the plan. To tiptoe into full-time. Until life threw a wrench.

In one day, I sent out resumes for ten different internships. The next day, I received a phone call from a Faraday Future recruiter. But they didn't want me for an internship in ten months. They wanted to hire me full-time as an engineer. Right now.

I said yes. Obviously.

They invited me to LA for an onsite technical interview. Standard stuff, like present something technical I'd worked on and field questions from the battery team. So, I flew down in my sharpest suit, thumb drive in my pocket. By that point, I'd given my research talk more times than I could count, so I didn't even bother practicing. There was no need.

After a quick round of intros, handshakes, and small talk, they gestured for me to start. I checked my watch. Took a breath. And launched in. I felt good. Solid. I watched the clock, adjusting my pace, and nailed the timing, aiming to hit fifteen minutes on the dot. I explained everything: my research, why it mattered, what I'd accomplished, what was left to do. No detail was skipped. No stone left unturned. And then—fifteen minutes flat—I landed the dismount.

"And with that, I thank you all for your attention. Any questions?"

In grad school, this would be the moment the floodgates opened. Hands would shoot up, students desperate to prove how smart they were. Usually it started hostile: "Can you go back four slides? I want to see that graph again. I think you're making a mistake there." And it always spiraled from there, with smart people eager to show off how much sharper they were than you. How much harder they'd scrutinized your data in ten minutes than you had in months.

At first, I didn't even notice how out-of-place I was with this talk. I was too wrapped up in the rhythm of my own voice; the polished delivery, the perfect pacing. But the furrowed brows and exchanged glances tipped me off.

No interruptions. No challenges. Just confusion. Silence.

That's when it hit me. This wasn't a research talk. This was an engineering interview. And I'd just burned fifteen minutes impressing absolutely nobody. The shame hit fast and hot. Flashbacks to previous failures flooded my brain. That NASA interview. The Ivy League situation.

I'm not a fit.

How could I be this dumb? Why hadn't I presented something else? A talk about wrenching on cars? Or some story about how much I loved LEGO as a kid? Sure, I couldn't share Tesla stuff because of the NDA, but still. What was I thinking?

Before I could spiral completely, someone finally spoke. "So ... you don't actually think this chemistry stuff applies to us, do you?"

It felt like an eternity as I stood there, trying to breathe. Trying to hold it together. First, my mind jumped back into that stairwell at UNR, listening to NASA's deafening silence. But then I remembered what I'd looked up afterward. And crying alone in that break room.

Lean into it. Be yourself, I reminded myself. My instinct screamed, *Backpedal. Explain. Salvage the moment.* But something quieter whispered back, *Just go with it. Dive into the mess.*

So I reached deep and pulled out the most honest thing I could muster. "I don't know. Does it?" When their confusion turned to surprise, I followed with, "When I applied for an internship next summer, I wasn't expecting to be asked if I wanted to work full time as an engineer. I don't really know why you want to hire me full-time."

That's when the interview began in earnest. They asked so many questions. I said "I don't know" more times than I ever had before. And I said "I can't answer that" more times than I expected to due to the NDA. Only one thing became clear: nobody in the room really knew what was expected of me. And it started to feel like the whole thing was slipping into a dead end.

Until one of them tossed out a curveball. "If you were going to buy solar panels and install them in your backyard, how would you figure out the best spot to put them?"

"I'd run the numbers, figure out three spots that get the most sun, and let my fiance pick between them hoping she didn't hate all three."

"But how do you know which spot is actually the best?"

"I don't. The best spot is the one she likes. No math will change that."

Silence. Then—laughter. Genuine, deep-belly laughter. I blinked. That wasn't the reaction I'd expected. And judging by how they laughed even harder when they saw the look on my face, it wasn't what they'd expected either.

We bounced through a few more light-hearted questions. Then quiet settled in, smiles lingering around the room.

The hiring manager leaned back, smirking. "Now it's our turn: Any questions for us?"

I hesitated. I had the floor again, finally. I could have played it safe. Asked about company culture, day-to-day stuff. I could have pretended I'd done a ton of research into the company, as if it was the only one I'd sent a resume to. But after everything that had just happened, what was the point of pretending?

So I just asked what was on my mind. "Yeah. Why is it that you're actually considering hiring me?"

The smiles faded. A few glances were passed around. The mood shifted, becoming heavier. There was a deeper truth they were avoiding. Something they were scared of. I'd touched on something real.

The hiring manager's smirk had vanished. "What do you know about thermal runaway?"

Oh, shit. Well, it was too late to back out now. And honesty was winning this back for me, so I couldn't start pretending now. "Practically nothing. That's when batteries blow up, right?"

He winced. "Okay. We can … work on that."

I walked out of that interview mostly just relieved. I'd fumbled, scrambled, and survived—again. Another moment I'd thought I was ready for. Another shameful surprise. Another lesson. NASA. The golf cart. A freaking tarantula. Now this. Different moments but the same gut punch.

At the time, I thought they were flukes. That my life was just a comedy. But they weren't. It isn't. It was something else entirely.

It was stupid questions. Reshaping my life.

GETTING BACK UP AFTER SHAME KNOCKS YOU DOWN.

16

THE RECOVERY

It's like walking through a spiderweb you didn't see. One second, you're striding forward, confident, eyes ahead. The next? You're flailing, scared, heart pounding. And then, as you realize someone might have seen you, the shame sets in.

That's exactly what it's like when you *accidentally* ask a stupid question. You freeze. Your brain scrambles. And then the shame hits like static in your chest. And for a split second, everything feels … wild. Unpredictable.

In these tangled moments, something strange happens. You're not just embarrassed. You're fully awake. The world feels too close, too loud. And in that raw exposure, there's power. Tap into it. Don't let it go to waste. Yes, 'power' is the *last* thing it feels like. But that's exactly why we need to talk about what happens next.

Let's be honest with ourselves. We spend so much of our life in routines. The 9 to 5's, the same shows, the same loops. Comfort zones that keep us settled. Keep us safe. But stupid questions—especially the ones you don't even realize are stupid questions until *after* they leave our mouths—snap us right out of that.

If you're like most people, you probably think you can avoid it if you simply work hard enough. *If I can do enough work, study hard enough, I will never be afraid to ask anything ever again. I'll get past it!* I'm sure you also thought you'd never walk into a spiderweb again.

You might think, *I've trained for this. I'll see it coming.* And then—WHACK. Shame all over again. And when this happens, you have to remember: stupidity isn't what lives at the heart of a stupid question. Courage is.

You aren't stupid because of that shame.

You. Are. Not.

I have repeated this to myself more times than I can count. And I only recently started to believe it.

> The sting of a stupid question has
> nothing to do with the question and
> everything to do with *you* making it
> through the shame you feel.

I've been doing this work for years. And still, sometimes I'll ask a question, hear the tiniest pause, and feel like I've blown it. Even though I *know* better. Even though I can tell myself in the moment, "That's applied shame" or "Hello again, my inner critic." It doesn't make the sting go away. Not instantly. It just gives me a way to deal with it.

It's *still* uncomfortable for me to recall that story about the Ivy Leaguers. Thinking about that tarantula crawling toward me *still* gives me chills. It would be very comfortable to forget about them both. But to forget is to decide to settle for comfort over growth. To forget, try to put it out of my mind, is to pretend the next spiderweb isn't there waiting for me to walk into it.

It takes strength to choose courage over comfort. And after you walk through one spiderweb, it takes courage to keep going. Because the next web might be another five feet in front of you, for all you know.

> The courageous part of Courageous
> Curiosity lies in the recovery. In
> not knowing what comes next but
> choosing to keep going.

I'm *not* saying you should sprint into every stupid question as fast as you can. Sometimes, what feels like progress is actually just panic. And even when you're good at bouncing back, you can only take so many hits. Because shame builds up. Fast. If you ask too many stupid questions in too short a time, even the strongest curiosity can start to buckle under the weight of the shame.

But that also doesn't mean to stop asking. It just means you need to know your limit.

I asked almost nobody anything in the week that followed that Model X door fiasco. Getting that close to being fired had me reeling, and it wasn't just my body that needed to recover. My inner kid did, too. All of me did.

The trick is to *notice* when you're close to your limit. And when you hit that point? Slow down. Pause. Let yourself recover before you dive back in. This isn't a race. It's a recovery. Respect your pace.

> There's a limit to how much shame
> you can absorb at once. Know your
> threshold and pace yourself.

When you finally stop to catch your breath, it's tempting to push everything down. But that's when you need to look closest. During this pause, you shouldn't avoid thinking about it. With recovery comes a pause from asking stupid questions, sure. But that doesn't mean *all* of you should pause.

During these periods is the perfect time to reflect. It's easy and natural to want to push past a shameful moment and forget it ever happened. But real growth comes from stopping long enough to ask yourself questions.

The pause isn't just for catching your breath. It's also for catching the lesson.

Whenever I'm still spinning from a recent shame spiral, these are some example questions I ask myself to anchor the moment:

- What / Who just triggered me?

- Did I learn something new?

- What kind of shame was that?

- Was that avoidable? *Should* it have been avoided?

That's been the key for me. After I froze in that conference room, I looked up 'How to introduce yourself to impressive people'. That's how I turned my botched interview with NASA into something useful. How I remembered it was okay to stand there at Faraday and say, "I don't know." Because it was the authentic me.

Reflection is what turned the mess into something useful. So leave room for it. Reflect. Personal reflection is where real recovery takes root. And where you turn scattered moments of shame into a map for growth. This reflection becomes your foundation. A habit you can build on. And once you've built this habit, you can start stretching your threshold too.

Because once you feel that rush—once you realize that stupid questions are *actually* a superpower—you'll want to ask more. And there's a way you can do that safely.

You can craft a curiosity comfort zone. It won't be a perfect place or a magic fix. But it will be space—or person, group, or habit—that makes it easier to ask the tough stuff. For me, it's been mentors who listen without judgement. Who'll answer honestly and with patience. For you, it might look different. But what matters, if you truly want to push that limit, is that you **have a place to practice**. A place where shame doesn't stick as easily. That's how you can build strength to carry the shame more easily the next time you step outside of your zone. Or the next time you're ripped out of it by a damn spiderweb you didn't see.

> If you want to ask more stupid questions, do it in a curiosity comfort zone. Where the sting of the shame hurts less.

There's another component to this still, though. Having this safe place to practice asking your stupid questions is important. But it's equally important that we don't try to short-circuit it with a quick fix.

Many of us have probably, at some point, gone to a chatbot as the recipient of our stupid question or ran to Reddit to hide behind a screen name when we ask. It's a tempting 'solution.' But don't make anonymous spaces your go-to. Why? Because the whole point is growth through ownership. And that growth comes when *you* stand there and own the moment, not when you throw it into a void and walk away. I felt stronger after I forgot how to introduce myself because I stayed in it. I felt stronger after that Faraday Future interview because I showed up fully, even though it was messy. I didn't have a handle to hide behind. Or a screen. It was just me. Asking. *That* is what builds the kind of strength that stays with you.

> Your curiosity comfort zone should have
> a human element to it, and it should
> be you—not an anonymous handle—
> asking it.

Online spaces can *supplement* your curiosity comfort zone, but they're not a replacement. They're too volatile. And the internet is its own kind of spiderweb. It looks inviting, until it flips. One moment things can seem helpful. The next? Dismissive, snarky, hostile.

I've fallen into that too, thinking I could ask anything, anywhere, and be fine. And yeah, sure, you might get answers. But that deeper growth? The resilience that sticks? It comes from asking as *yourself*, in real spaces, with real stakes. That's where the *real* power of courageous curiosity lives. The strongest curiosity comfort zones are where you ask boldly, as yourself.

> No matter how careful you are, you're going to ask another stupid question.

You'll freeze up. You'll feel that old sting. But that's not a sign of failure. That's the proof you're still moving. Still learning and brave enough to ask.

So, brush off the spiderweb and trust that you'll eventually learn how to make the flailing look like dancing. Then take a breath. Because the best thing you can do isn't dodge the next spiderweb. It's to head straight into it, knowing full-well that it's right there.

Like I did. By accepting the role of battery engineer at Faraday Future. Without having the first clue what engineering even was.

WHEN YOU THOUGHT YOU WERE IN A PLACE OF COMFORT BUT REALIZE YOU WERE WRONG.

17

THE OVERSIGHT

"What's a busbar?" I asked, loud enough to cut through the room. I leaned back like it was nothing, expecting a simple answer. Instead, I received silence. In place of words, every head had turned, eyes squinted. *Oh no.*

I'd gotten that job at Faraday Future. I started working there full time just a few weeks after the interview. The technical learning curve was one thing. But the *real* shock to my system was the utter lack of privacy. There was nowhere to hide your mistakes. No way to whisper a stupid question without an audience. Everything was open. Hundreds of people had line-of-sight to my computer screen at all times. Every conversation was public. I could see the CEO standing at his desk from mine. The pressure to *always* be "on mission" was constant.

I learned fast that I would never be able to work on my PhD at the office.

By the time I'd asked this question, it was February 2017. I'd been pulling double duty—full-time engineer by day, PhD candidate by night—for months. My days were a blur of questions, CAD designs, and frantic notetaking as I scrambled to figure out how batteries worked and how engineers were *supposed* to work. And my nights were spent buried in dissertation chapters, chasing down experiments I had to re-run, and planning my next flight back to Reno to run it.

Two worlds with zero overlap.

Nobody understood why I did it. The chemists at UNR all thought I was only pursuing the engineering job to escape the shame of what happened with my first advisor, but they had no idea how chronically scared I was that engineering might not work out and I might need the PhD later. The engineers at Faraday Future were impressed with my depth in chemistry knowledge, but they had no idea about what had happened with my first advisor in graduate school. Each side only knew half the picture, and that made my time with each group equally lonely. No matter which group I was with, I had something to hide.

Both groups asked me the same question. "Why even bother finishing your PhD? There's no need."

I spared both groups the story. "I'm relentless." It was always easy to hide the truth behind that.

The people around me at the office were the smartest engineers I'd ever met. Even my immediate desk buddies were impressive enough. On the one side sat a Boeing vet who'd essentially memorized the 140-page document for how to drill a hole. On the other, was a helicopter designer so sharp, he never spoke unless it mattered. I was in the deep end. And that was just my immediate neighbors. The further you got from my desk—toward the CEO's—the brainpower only got heavier.

The guy who sat behind me became a lifeline. He had a master's in material science, a calm way about him, and a thousand-yard stare that told me he'd done his time in the lab, just like me. We clicked instantly; same background, same language. But he was also patient. Patient in a way that made it feel *safe* to ask him anything.

I saved every stupid question for him. It didn't take long to figure out I could trust him with all of it, no matter how stupid. And eventually, we reached a point where I wouldn't even turn around. I'd just blurt something out, and he'd quietly spin his chair, glance at my screen, and answer. There was never any eye rolling or deep sighs. He would just answer, as if it were the most natural thing in the world.

It was because of him that I'd started to *appreciate* the open office lay-out. Not for the noise—God, the noise was awful—but for the speed. Instant help anytime I needed it.

By now, that was my rhythm. Sit down. Struggle. Ask a question. Get the help I needed. Repeat. I'd been worried at first, paranoid that the other engineers, the brilliant people all around me, were secretly clock-ing every dumb thing I asked. But they kept their headphones on, laser-focused on their work, and after a while, I'd let myself believe they couldn't hear me. That as long as the headphones were on, I was invisible. So, I started to let my guard down.

For weeks, something had been bugging me. I *knew* what a busbar was. Technically. A stiff piece of metal connecting different parts of a battery. But what I couldn't figure out was why the name? It sounded ridiculous. A bus moves people around. What did that have to do with batteries? Why not just call it a current bar or something less weird? It struck me as odd.

So, one afternoon, I leaned back in my chair, casual as ever, and said, "What's a busbar?" And just like always, I expected my friend to turn, glance, answer, and move on. Instead, everything stopped. The hum of conversations, the click of keyboards—gone.

I looked around. Every engineer in earshot, including ones who had *never* acknowledged I existed, were locked on me now. I froze. Weren't they all listening to music? Or Podcasts? It hit me, mid-panic: the headphones were just props. A false wall. I'd mistaken quiet for safety, and that was my real oversight.

"... Because it shuttles the current back and forth between charge and discharge."

I blinked. And turned my gaze back to my friend. "Ohhh, so it's like a bus for electrons?"

He nodded. "Yeah. Engineers are weird about naming things."

And that should have been it. A simple question, a simple answer. But no one else moved. The stares stayed. I'd stepped on something sacred. Engineers don't just *name* things. They *define* things. And questioning that, out loud, was apparently taboo.

I inhaled and ignored the death stares. "Okay, thanks. That makes sense. But what about current-carrying cables? Are those called busbars too?"

"Depends how it's connected. Busbars are usually bolted in; cables get clipped with connectors. If it's a flexible busbar, we just call it that."

"Awesome, thank you!" I said, some relief finally settling into my gut. "The boss asked me to categorize all the parts in the battery. This clears that up a ton."

He nodded and turned back to his screen.

I exhaled, ready to move on, but then I heard furious typing. From every engineer around me. And minutes later, my inbox started pinging with detailed lists, part numbers, subcategories, acronyms I'd never seen. It was like I'd accidentally kicked a hornet's nest of helpfulness. Every part in the battery was broken down line by line in a few minutes, categorized to death.

One email, from the busbar engineer, ended with a note: "*No flexible busbars. No need for that shit. We know how to handle tolerances.*"

I stared at it, baffled. What did *tolerances* have to do with flexible busbars? I didn't know. But if I'd learned anything, it was that sometimes, asking feels just as dangerous as not asking. So, this time, I didn't hesitate. I hit reply. And started typing, a smile tugging at my lips.

This was becoming fun.

WHEN SOMEONE RIPS DOWN EVERY WALL YOU HAVE, BEGGING YOU TO GO AWAY.

18

THE PANIC

I was certain he was stonewalling. But I still told myself, *he's just tired. He'll come around.* And asked again, "Where's your ADV plan?" Seconds later, I was in the middle of a full-blown panic attack.

There was one person at Faraday Future I couldn't avoid. I was in charge of picking the fluid to cool the battery. He was in charge of picking the pump to move it. We were stuck with each other. If he didn't know the fluid, he couldn't pick the pump. If I didn't know the pump, I couldn't pick the fluid.

I liked working with him at first. If you'd spent a day with him and guessed his job, you'd probably say guitarist in a Grateful Dead cover band. His vibe was pure Jerry Garcia. It reminded me of my brother—same grin, same no-big-deal energy. Which made it easy to trust him. Maybe too easy. But it was also … different.

There was this weird friction from day one. Every question I asked about the pump got deflected or dodged. It felt personal, even though

I didn't want to believe it. But it was hard not to. Everywhere else in the company—roughly 1,500 people—answers came back fast. Crystal clear. Or at least that's how it felt. But none of that mattered this day.

The day before, I'd gotten the email: my PhD was officially complete. No more writing my dissertation in that basement after hours huffing chemicals. No more flights to Reno. My diploma was in the mail. I'd finally earned it. Dr. Cournoyer. My wife and a bunch of friends from work celebrated at a bar with a tab we didn't close until late. I was flying high that day, even if a bit hungover. And work was going *super* well, too. I'd finished everything; scanned the entire marketplace, tested every type of cooling fluid I could find, met with every single major supplier, mapped the whole thing in CAD—fluid paths, pump points, every last detail. I'd even run thermal calculations with the analysis engineer—checked, double-checked. And everyone agreed: it worked. Even my boss had signed off on it and said he'd seen pumps that could handle it, even if only barely. I'd gotten his tentative approval.

We'd checked every single box. I was *this* close to releasing my first-ever part for a production vehicle. It felt incredible. Everything was clicking at that moment. And yet, something felt off. Like I was waiting for a punch I couldn't see coming. And I knew it had something to do with the *single* box left to check.

I still needed to know what pump we were going to use.

He'd taken longer and longer to respond to emails. And he'd gotten harder and harder to find. Details escaped his every reply. It messed with my head. Was it coincidence? Was I overthinking? Was he mad I hadn't included him enough? Jealous? I'd never once considered the simplest explanation, that maybe the guy I'd thought I knew wasn't the guy I'd thought I knew. That his easy-going vibe might not have been who he was at all. That maybe it was just a mask I hadn't realized I'd mistaken for truth.

So, on this day, given my high-flying state of mind, I decided he was probably just overworked. The battery team's director of test and validation had asked me to put together an "ADV" plan—Analysis, Development, and Validation. Basically, a giant list. Every single test needed to prove a part could survive the life of a vehicle. But before I even started it, I figured, why not offer to help the pump engineer?

I knew where he might be. Downstairs in the prototype garage, probably running yet another test on the vehicle that always seemed to eat up all his time. As I walked up, I spotted him at a desk, casually scrolling through something on his computer. But the second he saw me coming? Boom. He sprang into action, grabbing a wrench and sliding under the car like his life depended on it.

Weird. Either he's *super* busy or trying *really* hard to avoid me. I gave him the benefit of the doubt. "Hey," I said, cheerful, "I'm about to start my ADV plan, but thought I could help you with yours too, if you want?"

"It's already done."

His flat, dismissive tone threw me. "Oh, wow. Okay. Where is it? Can I take a look? It would help me figure out how much fluid you'll need so I can get it ordered."

Silence. He kept wrenching.

I glanced at his screen; he'd been looking at test results for a different fluid. The one we'd *already* ruled out. Weird. "Hey, did you hear me? Where's your ADV plan? I'll actually need to see it to work on mine." Still nothing. So I waited. Then, thinking maybe he just didn't realize how much this was holding me up, I added, "I need to see it to finalize the fluid selec—"

He shot up and hurled the wrench onto the floor. "GET THE FUCK AWAY FROM ME! YOU'RE SUCH A *MORON*. WHAT THE FUCK EVEN IS AN ADV PLAN? YOU'RE ALWAYS MAKING UP THIS STUPID SHIT. YOU HAVE NO FUCKING CLUE WHAT YOU'RE DOING. GET THE FUCK OUT OF HERE!"

I'd braced for resistance. A brush-off, maybe. But this? My ears rang. My face went hot. My heart slammed inside my chest, and my throat cinched shut like a fist was closing around it. I couldn't think. Couldn't stop my hands from shaking. My body was hijacked, and I had zero control.

I bolted. Out of the building, I willed my legs into the nearby test bunker, and let my body do whatever it needed to. After what felt like an eternity, air finally found its way into my lungs again. The choking slowed, and the shaking started to calm a bit. Then my voice came back—albeit, as a whimper. And finally, my brain.

I'd *thought* that was a safe question. A simple one. A necessary one. But that was the mistake. I'd assumed logic would win. Instead, I'd stepped onto an invisible landmine.

That's when I noticed someone else in the room. A technician I knew. He'd been standing there the whole time. Frozen. Watching me unravel.

He waited a second. Then, gently asked, "Hey … do you want a hug?"

I blinked. Then laughed. He laughed too. And just like that, the world was okay again. Not fixed, but okay.

That was the day after I'd officially earned my PhD. The day after I'd finally gotten the thing I'd worked so hard for. But the funny thing is, it was never about the PhD. What mattered—what *still* matters—is every time I stood back up after taking the risk and asking the stupid question.

WHEN YOUR STUPID QUESTION ISN'T A QUESTION; IT'S AN ASSUMPTION.

19

THE ASSUMPTION

"Is 7:00 A.M. too late?" I asked, then added quickly, "I can do 6:00 A.M. if that's better."

His face tightened, but I couldn't understand why. Did I say something wrong? Did the screen freeze?

By my one-year mark at Faraday Future, I felt like I had the whole thing down. I knew *everything* about the fluid we were using to cool the battery. Well, everything except who we would actually buy it from. I'd tested every option so thoroughly, I could probably have reverse-engineered the formulas myself. Once we'd picked the winning fluid—the one that checked every box—I wrote up a specification and blasted it out to every supplier I could think of, hoping to reel one in.

Most responses were easy to dismiss; sales reps pushing their own "special" fluids for all the wrong reasons. But a few were solid. And one stood out above the rest: eager, aggressive, and downright *hungry* for the business. They were based in the UK. And to prove their commitment, they flew to California for our first meeting without hesitation. They also came in hot with their pricing. It wasn't even a contest.

I'd never worked with an international supplier before, so it was a little bumpy at first. When they asked to set up a regular project sync, I casually threw out 1:00 P.M. as a proposed time. They laughed. Turns out, 1:00 P.M. California time is 9:00 P.M. UK time. Oops. I apologized. They did too, for laughing. We landed on 8:00 AM Tuesdays, California time.

My contact was okay with an end-of-day meeting at 4:00 PM his time. I was just relieved I wouldn't have to drag myself in any earlier.

It was around this time I got handed another project: designing the plastic isolation for the high-voltage busbars in the battery pack. They're the snap-on plastic caps that cover the terminals, basically the only thing stopping you from accidentally zapping yourself.

The design had been started by another engineer, who'd since quit. My job was to finish it. But the supplier had already been picked, even though the design wasn't done. Total opposite of how I'd handled the fluid project. And said supplier was based in China.

After my rocky start with the UK team, you'd think I'd have learned a thing or two about time zone etiquette by now. Nope. When I emailed the main contact at the Chinese company and asked if he wanted to meet "after lunch" for a regular weekly tag-up, he wrote back, *"The earliest we can is 6:00 P.M. your time. Our plant is just starting up then. Tuesday morning is our only availability."*

That was when I walked my dogs, so I mentioned that the LA traffic would likely be heard in the background and I'd be on my phone instead of my computer, but he said he was fine with it. So that became our routine.

Tuesdays became a whole experience of their own. In the office early for the UK fluid meeting, and in the evening, out with the dogs, phone pressed to my ear, talking plastic parts and draft angles with China while I picked up dog poop. I was convinced Tuesdays had a personal vendetta against me.

A few months later, my boss decided we needed a backup fluid supplier. I dug up the old list and found my second-favorite company, based in France. I checked their site, praying for a US satellite office. No dice. But I emailed them anyway, figuring they'd reply at midnight. Sure enough, I got a response at 12:14 in the morning. But instead of the dreaded 6:00 or 7:00 A.M. meeting request, they offered 9:00 A.M. Beautiful.

I'd expected a groggy early-morning scramble or, worse, a delay of a few days. Instead, I got to sleep in *and* keep momentum.

I felt like a seasoned pro at juggling global schedules. So when I dialed into the meeting, I figured I knew exactly how it was going to go. But I was wrong. Sure, at first, everything about the meeting went as expected. But as we wrapped up, the supplier said, "Alright, we should set up a regular weekly chat as things move forward. Tuesdays work best for me. How about you?"

I didn't laugh, but I definitely clocked the pattern, and decided it was better not to fight it. "Sure. Tuesdays work. Is 7:00 A.M. too late?" I was proud of myself for nailing the global-time-zone thing by this point. "I can make 6:00 A.M. work if needed."

I was greeted by silence. A long, heavy silence.

I frowned at the screen. Did the call drop?

Then came the sharp reply. "Listen, I know France has a bit of a reputation, but there's no need to talk down to me. I *offered* to meet at this time today. Do you not think we're capable of adjusting our schedules to meet yours?"

My brain scrambled. What reputation? What was he talking about? I ran through everything I could think of about French stereotypes and came up blank. Was he insulted? I was too blindsided to be offended. "Wait, what reputation? I don't ... I don't understand. What do you mean?" More silence. I figured he was measuring whether I was messing with him or not. So I let the silence sit for a moment before adding, "So, do you want to meet later then?"

Of all the supplier meetings I'd had up to that point, I never expected the most delicate negotiation to be over meeting times. The shame was there, but mostly, I was just confused.

He finally said, "Let's just keep the 9:00 A.M. slot, if that's okay."

That night, I told Emily—now my wife—the whole story. She didn't even blink. "Yeah," she said flatly. "I've heard French people are super touchy about working late. And there's some kind of law about having to take an hour-long lunch break."

Ah. Mystery solved. Oops. I'd thought stupid questions were about knowledge gaps. Turns out, sometimes they're just about stepping on invisible cultural landmines. Still, I was relieved. I wouldn't have to wake up earlier after all on Tuesdays. Or so I thought.

At midnight, my phone dinged. *Here we go.* I groaned and rolled over, squinting at the screen. *"Does your offer to have our weekly meeting at 6:00 A.M. still stand?"*

I dropped my head back onto the pillow and sighed. My Tuesdays had just got longer. And once again, I'd received proof that just when you think you've got it all figured out, there's always another spiderweb waiting for you to stroll right into it.

WHEN THE QUESTION ISN'T YOUR PROBLEM, YOUR TIMING IS.

20

THE CONFUSION

The company was falling apart around me. But I was too busy discovering something incredible to notice. Something new. Something exciting. "Can we add this to the battery?" I asked, barely containing myself.

As 2017 wound down, things at Faraday Future were grim. Rumors swirled nonstop about the company running out of money. Losing our jobs felt inevitable. My boss—who used to be glued to his desk, always available—grew more distracted by the day. And the execs had abandoned their open-office seats long ago. Now, they spent their days holed up in glass-walled conference rooms, red-faced, yelling at each other and leaving the rest of us confused.

Day by day, we were getting less guidance, less direction. Approvals for basic things started taking forever. We all felt it. And my boss might as well have become a ghost. Meetings went unattended. Emails were met with radio silence. I was hearing more from the other engineers about today's tasks than him. But weirdly, I wasn't worried. Not yet anyway.

While everyone else was caught up in the chaos, I stayed locked in and on mission. By then, I'd been asked to finish designing a few more parts, one of which was the thermal barrier between battery modules. We were using mica. Pretty standard stuff. Basically a rock shredded and mashed together into thin sheets. And at first, it seemed a simple enough part to figure out. But the deeper I dug, curiosity fully engaged, the more questions I had.

How did mica actually *work*? What was it actually made of? And was there a cheaper alternative? Because, honestly, it seemed absurdly expensive for glorified rock paper.

As I kept digging into thermal barriers, reading more about it each day, I stumbled across something *wild*. There was this thing called "intumescent materials." I clicked a video, curious to learn more. And when I watched it, all I could think was, *whoa*. It looked like a flimsy sheet of cardboard. But when the guy hit it with a torch, it *expanded*. And kept expanding. And expanding. What started as a wafer-thin piece turned into a giant black char nearly 5-inches tall.

I sat there, stunned. Then I checked the price. Pennies on the dollar compared to the mica. Sold. I snapped into execution mode and called a sales rep. Samples were on the way to our address within minutes.

A few days later, I had the torch in hand, same as the video, and ran the test in front of the battery safety test team. Their jaws dropped too. Not only was this stuff a thermal barrier, but as it expanded, it sealed every air gap between the modules, locking everything down even tighter. Safer. And as an added bonus, the char was soft, so there was no pressure build up risk.

In the end, I talked the guy down to a piece price 1/10th of the mica. I'd hit a total home run in under a week.

I threw together a deck and sent it to my boss with a calendar invite. No response. The meeting time came and went. I swung by his desk—empty. Again and again. Two weeks passed. The holidays were looming, and I knew people would vanish soon. So, I sent a high-priority email.

Finally, he bit. *"Sure, let's talk."*

We sat down in a conference room. I ran through everything at warp speed, buzzing with energy. "So, can we add this to the battery?" I asked at the end. "At first, I thought just a straight swap for the mica, but honestly, I think we could deploy this in a few other spots too." I was practically vibrating with excitement. As I pitched, I was already drafting the victory email in my head. "I was reading that in construction, they add this stuff to door frames so it seals up tight during a fire. That same mentali—"

He raised a hand, eyes shut and shaking his head. "Who else have you told about this?"

Of *all* the reactions I'd prepared for, that was not on the list. I blinked. "Uh, a few of the battery test guys. And a couple other engineers. That's it, I think?"

Relief flooded his face. He nodded. "Yeah, no. We're not adding this. Delete the presentation. Toss the samples. No more discussion." And then—that *look*. What was that? A wink? No, not quite. But it was something. Something knowing. Like an inside joke that everyone was in on but me, and I was the punchline.

Before I could ask about it, he was up and out the door. Practically skipping. Light on his feet in a way I hadn't seen in weeks. Like he'd just scored a win I didn't yet understand.

I sat there, hollow. Confused. Mad. Sad. All of it, but mostly just baffled. This was a *great* idea. It deserved an answer. Why trash it? Why kill it completely? And why did he look so damn pleased?

The whole thing churned in my brain for days. It didn't add up. Until he quit. On the same day as the rest of the senior engineering crew. The same day as the CFO. And the CTO. Gone. And within days, a rival EV company popped up. Their headquarters was literally down the street from Faraday Future. And the founders were made up of everyone who'd left. My boss. Our old CFO. CTO.

That's what that look had been. It hit me like a slap in the face. That look hadn't been confusion. It had been a silent message. *Bury this. We'll use it at the next place.* At least, that's what I reasoned. It was the only way I could make sense of it.

Eventually, I got a new boss. And the first thing I did was request a meeting. I dropped the whole story on him; the deck, the demo, and the weird not-quite-wink my prior boss had given me. Then I asked, "So, can we add this to the battery?"

He leaned back. "It's interesting. Really smart. Let's get the lawyers involved to make sure we patent the idea, especially in case they try to run off with it. Beyond that? It's honestly probably too late in the cycle now to implement for FF91. But we'll keep it on deck for the next vehicle architecture. Nice work."

A patent? That caught me. All at once, the weight of that hit like an elephant parking on my chest. Images of Edison and Tesla flashed through my brain. The patent wars. Ownership battles. Suddenly, I saw it all in a new light.

My new boss—calm, casual—was probably right. And my *old* boss? I couldn't help but flash back to almost exactly a year earlier, when the same guy, with the same sharp stare, grilled me in my interview: "*What do you know about thermal runaway?*" Back then? Not much. Now? I'd just handed him the answer. But that same guy was gone now and was probably already drafting his own patent.

That was a really hard truth to stomach. Was he a friend? Foe? Was I supposed to follow him?

I exhaled, anchoring myself in the moment. "Okay. So, uh ... how do I file a patent?" I'd thought I was solving a basic engineering problem, finding a no-brainer solution. *Can we make the product better?* But now, I understood. That was never the question. The real question was, *Who gets there first?* I'd just been caught in the crossfire.

WHEN THE FLINCH FADES AND THE FEAR BECOMES YOUR COMPASS.

21

THE EDGE

You know that feeling when you add just a little too much weight to the dumbbell for the lift? Not enough to fail, but enough that everything shakes, and you realize you're at your edge? That's exactly what it's like when you ask a stupid question on purpose. You walk right up to the border of what feels safe and push.

They say, *"Life begins at the edge of your comfort zone."* It sounds bold and clean. But life starts *inside* your comfort zone. That's where you learn. Where you find your footing. Where you build the base to be able to move out of your comfort zone later.

Life starts in your comfort zone. Growth starts at its edge. The hard part is finding that edge and going there enough times and long enough to grow. Push too hard, too fast, and you panic instead. Ask a question too raw, too heavy, and you crash from the weight of the shame.

It happened to me. When I asked that co-worker about his ADV plan, a part of me knew I should have tread more carefully. But I didn't want to wait. I wanted to push more than I could lift. And I paid the consequences.

That's not where learning lives. The goal in finding the edge—in asking stupid questions on purpose—is discomfort. Not panic.

There's an easy trick to landing in discomfort. Especially when the shame behind the question is applied. Let people know you're still learning. A simple, "I know this might be basic, but ..." makes all the difference. It signals honesty. I should have said it. It sets expectations clearly. It keeps the conversation grounded. It keeps things in check for you and for them.

That is why my boss's comment at Tesla saved me. "He's just an intern." It had always been a way of saying, "Hey, he doesn't have an agenda. He honestly just wants to know. He's new here."

> Set the stage with honest vulnerability
> before asking stupid questions on
> purpose.

You might reason you can hand off your question to someone else. Ask them to lift the weight for you. We all try it at some point because it feels safer and cleaner. And sure, there's value in *watching* someone else do something. Once. So you can learn. But you don't need more examples.

That's why I've included so many in this book. There's no growth in watching more examples from the sidelines. You won't get any stronger by watching someone else lift. You have to step up to the bench yourself. You have to put in the reps.

I shouldn't have asked my friend what a busbar was. I should have started with the busbar engineer. But I'd wanted someone else to do the work for me, and I ended up working with that engineer anyway. The time in between had just been wasted.

> You can't build strength by outsourcing
> your stupid questions. Ask them yourself
> so you get to grow through the shame.

I tried to perfect a question, only to turn it into a stupid question in the process. I was *so* confident that I knew how to talk to that Frenchman. The delivery was perfect. It was my Faraday Future interview all over again. But all that perfecting isn't being "thorough." It's just stalling. And that's the hidden trap: we convince ourselves that a better-worded question will feel less shameful. But it won't.

That call with the supplier in France was a perfect moment to bond with honesty. Instead, I hid behind perfection. Imagine how the story would have played out if I'd been honest. "Okay, so we need to plan a meeting time. I have yet to get this right, so hopefully, I get it right this time. Let me tell you a story or two…"

There's no perfect way to ask. There's only asking. Or staying silent.

> Don't stall by making your question
> perfect before asking it. Just get it out
> there.

There are times when you *know* you should ask, but you talk yourself out of it. This one's sneaky. You start thinking, *This question is too simple. Too obvious. I shouldn't even need to ask.* So you hold back for longer than you should. Like I did with the idea that became my first patent. A part of me knew I was giving my boss too much leniency, that he was shirking his responsibilities. I should have pushed harder. Made more noise.

You're the only one who knows what's obvious to you. And nobody else is living your learning journey. There's no such thing as a simple question. And the "simple" questions—the ones you're most embarrassed to ask—are often the ones that unlock the biggest breakthroughs.

> No question is too simple if it fills a gap
> for you. So ask it.

Just like with lifting weights, this process gets easier. With every rep, every question, the fear morphs into something else. It doesn't disappear, but you recognize it. It feels comfortable. The muscle builds. And your edge starts moving farther and farther out.

What felt risky last month might feel natural today. That's the proof you're leveling up. And every time you step up, you reinforce it. You tell your brain, *I'm not tiny. I'm someone who grows. I'm someone who does hard things.* That's the real change.

And sure, there is tremendous personal value in that change. You will benefit greatly as you continue to ask stupid questions wisely, but when you get to the point of Courageous Curiosity where you know how to wield stupid questions like a professional, new doors open up too. It's not just that you will start to grow, but you'll start to notice how you can use your own stupid questions to help others grow, too.

WHEN
SHARED
DISCOMFORT
SAYS MORE
THAN THE
CORRECT
ANSWER EVER
COULD.

22

THE CONNECTION

"What's I^2R?" I asked. Everyone in earshot burst out laughing. He didn't. I didn't. We just looked at each other. I smiled. I was comfortable here. He wasn't. Yet.

When I was furloughed from Faraday Future in November 2018, I'd made a vow, both to myself and to Emily: never again. Never another half-baked startup. I was done with the chaos. The whiplash leadership changes. The total lack of direction. The creeping sense that no one really knew what we were supposed to be doing. That chapter was closed.

Then a recruiter had emailed me about an open house at another no-name EV company. A stealth startup. I'd hovered over the delete button but hesitated.

I'd mentioned it over dinner, and Emily didn't even look up from her plate. "You don't have a job." Then she *did* look up, and the reminder was clear in her glare. Our first kid was due in 5 months.

The next day, I was in bumper-to-bumper traffic on the 405 in LA, grumbling to myself the whole way, convinced this was going to be a total waste of time. But as soon as I'd walked through the doors, I'd felt lighter. It had only been a few weeks since the layoffs, but seeing everyone I'd worked with again, it felt like coming up for air. Smiles everywhere. Laughs. People swapping job search horror stories, bonding over rejection emails and half-baked interviews.

For a minute, I'd let myself soak it in. It was a relief to forget about being unemployed, even if only for a moment. But then I saw it. A binder on a table. The company's *101* manual. My eyes had locked on, and everything else blurred out. *Probably just corporate fluff,* I'd thought. Another "synergy and innovation" mission statement, blah, blah, blah. But my curiosity won.

I'd picked it up and flipped through it. I hadn't expected much. But my hands moved faster the deeper into the manual I'd went. It spelled everything out: why their product mattered, who they needed, what problems they were solving and how they were solving them. Every question I'd asked at Faraday Future but never got a straight answer to was right here in plain English.

And as I'd kept reading, I'd found stuff I hadn't even *thought* to ask back at Faraday Future:

- What kind of employees do we need to hire right now?

- What kind of employees are we *avoiding* right now?

- What problems are staring us in the face, and how will you help us solve them?

I'd kept turning pages, stunned, not just by how complete the manual was but by how *clear* it was. Whoever had put that thing together knew *exactly* what they were doing.

By the time I'd closed that binder, my mind had been made up. I *had* to work there. That company was going to *crush* it, and I'd wanted in.

When my turn came up to interview with the battery team lead, I'd walked in and pointed at the binder. "I just read that whole thing. And I'm telling you, you need me here. You guys are going to win. And I know exactly how to help."

They'd skimmed my resume and asked a couple of quick questions. But it hadn't taken long before they cut to the chase: "How soon can you start?"

I'd driven home floating. I couldn't believe it. When I'd gotten home and told Emily, she thought I'd gone nuts for going against my promise, but this was an opportunity that just felt right. She was too curious not to ask, "So…what's the name of the company?" I shrugged and told her, "Some stupid made-up name that makes no sense. Rivian?"

A few weeks later, I sat at my new desk, riding high. This was it. No more chaos. No more uncertainty. No more wasted time. I was convinced that everyone there *got it*. Everyone spoke with clarity. Everyone knew the mission. No more guessing. No more shaming. Just solid work getting done.

Then the door slammed open. A guy stormed in, muttering under his breath about his Porsche breaking down. He tossed stuff onto his desk like he owned the place and didn't even look my way. And I knew immediately what kind of person he was. The type who *always* had the answers. The smartest guy in the room. The guy who radiated expertise and left a wake of shame for everyone else. By now, I could spot that person a mile away, and these were the people I'd spent my whole career dodging. Until now.

Right on cue, he looked around the room and said loudly, "Can you believe those interviews from Faraday Future? Half of them didn't even know what I^2R is."

Worried, I slid my headphones on, pretending to work while I listened in.

He continued, "You should never be allowed to work on a battery if you don't know what I^2R is."

At that, my new boss smirked at me. And right then, I had a choice to make. Hide or ask. Because no, I had no idea what I^2R was. Not yet.

I sighed. I already knew what I had to do. No point putting it off. So I pulled off my headphones and took a deep breath. I looked straight at that engineer and said: "What's I^2R?"

For a second, the room froze. Then, laughter exploded. The engineer chuckled at first, assuming I was joking. But when I raised my eyebrows, dead serious, his smile faltered. Soured.

He shot back, "Power. Who are you?"

My boss cut in, still grinning, "He's one of the Faraday guys from the open house. We just hired him."

The laughter roared even louder. And just like that, the illusion shattered. This wasn't going to be some perfect utopia of clarity and knowledge. I was still going to be *that guy*, the one asking the questions nobody else had to. I would *always* be that guy. It stung. But I smiled anyway. Because in that moment, I caught his face, that engineer who would become one of my closest friends. He looked hurt too. We both felt it. Both took the hit. But that hit, that awful flash of shame, is what made the connection stick.

WHEN YOU TAKE THE HIT SO SOMEONE ELSE DOESN'T HAVE TO.

23

THE DEFIANCE

The silence stretched. My hands curled into fists under the table. My face went cold. My body braced. I wasn't supposed to push back. I knew it. We all did. We could feel it in the way the room froze and the air thickened. The smart move was shutting up. But that wasn't going to stop me. I never do the smart thing.

I took a deep breath. "Why not?"

Things at Rivian went really well for me—until they didn't. The trouble started when the company began shifting its center of gravity from Michigan to Southern California. At first, Rivian was mostly a Michigan-based company. Almost everyone worked there, except for me and the battery team. We were the outliers working in SoCal. And whenever people from Michigan visited our tiny little office, they would joke about how silly we looked, all on our headsets talking to the team in Michigan.

They nicknamed our building 'The Call Center'. We didn't care. We had an edge they didn't see coming; the time zone difference.

At first, it drove my teammates nuts. They'd show up at 9:00 A.M., and would only get a couple of hours of overlap with Michigan before everyone in Michigan was done for the day. I was different. My commute was brutal, so I'd started making it into the office by 6:00 A.M. to dodge the LA traffic. And as it turned out, that lined up perfectly. By the time I'd roll in, the Michigan team was just sitting at their desks to start the day too.

For months, I'd been the only one in the SoCal office until 8:00 A.M. And in that quiet, a habit formed. Every morning, I'd check in with Michigan. I'd get a pulse check. I'd catch them right after their daily standup, and they'd fill me in on new marching orders from the execs, today's biggest problems, shifts in the schedule, or what was going sideways. And in return, I'd give them updates they'd missed after hours, everything the SoCal team had cranked out while the Michigan team had been home having dinner or putting the kids to bed.

This routine had turned me into the person who always knew what was *really* going on. I had my finger on the company's pulse in a way nobody else in the SoCal office did. If anyone wanted the latest scoop, they'd come to me. And it got to the point where, in meetings, I'd chime in like clockwork: "Well, Michigan said they're behind too, so there's no point burning ourselves out trying to hit a deadline they won't either."

The engineers *loved* it. The program managers? Not so much. Except one.

Our battery team's program manager had moved her desk *right* next to mine early on. Every morning, coffee in hand, she'd sit down and ask, "So, what's the latest?" She wouldn't boss us around. She'd just gather the facts and relay them to her boss and the other PMs.

Whenever someone higher up pushed back on her, she'd check in with me. "I'm hearing Michigan says they can go faster now. Should we ramp up to meet their pace?"

And I'd respond simply, "Nope. My top sources told me yesterday that they're still behind. If we rush, all we'll do is clog up our floor space waiting for them to catch up."

Thanks to her—and thanks to those daily syncs—the battery team gained a reputation. Frustratingly on time and never late but rarely early. And that didn't sit well with some of my Michigan buddies.

They'd started slipping me bad info, hoping to trip us up and make us look bad for a change. So I'd made more friends. Asked more questions. Tightened my circle of trust. And when the company started hiring like crazy, I'd hustled to meet every new face before Michigan had a chance to sour them against me.

The battery team had stayed solid. And after a while, I didn't just know what was happening in Michigan. I knew what was coming, sometimes before Michigan even saw it themselves. I could sniff out real updates from program management spin without breaking a sweat. Then it happened. The day we in SoCal had seen coming, but Michigan hadn't.

The CEO had announced that the company's headquarters would be moving to Southern California. The Michigan office had been shrinking, fast. He'd framed it gently, said Orange County would be the company's new "center of gravity," but the message had been clear: If they wanted to stay with the company, they were moving west. It hit the Michigan team hard. But those of us in SoCal had mostly shrugged. It didn't seem like much would change for us.

But we were wrong. So wrong.

Just a few days later, a new guy had shown up at the office. He'd already gotten to his desk when I'd arrived at 6:00. And everything about him screamed VP: shoulders back, eyes sharp, scanning the room like he owned it. And the desk he had picked? Directly in front of mine.

We'd gotten to talking, and after a few questions, I'd pegged him fast. He was the guy. The one who'd been pushing from a distance, pressuring us to move faster. Our program manager's boss, maybe even her boss's boss.

I'd kept it casual but couldn't help asking, "So, you checking in before our next milestone, or what?"

He'd smiled and said the worst thing he could have. "Nope. This is my new home. We're starting the transition to make this HQ."

At first, I'd told myself he was just settling in. Refused to believe it.

Day one, day two; I'd kept watch. By day three, I knew better. He hadn't just been listening. He'd been logging. His eyes had tracked every conversation like a hawk, fingers flying across his laptop now and then. He hadn't moved to our office to learn. He'd arrived to take over.

It started slow. At first, I'd just take my calls somewhere else. I'd slip into conference rooms and keep my voice low. The updates I'd gave Michigan turned into texts. Then emails. Anything to keep them out of his ears. But I could still feel it; him listening, watching, tracking every move, learning how we worked, just waiting to tear it all apart.

Then the day came. The moment I'd been dreading. Our program manager turned to me and asked, "Hey Travis, what's the latest out of

Michigan? Do you think they're going to hit this latest timing?"

My stomach clenched. I could feel him listening. And sure enough, he cut in fast and sharp. "Excuse me, why would you ask him that?"

She blinked, flustered. "I, um ... well, I just—"

"Michigan is on schedule. Don't ask him those kinds of questions. You can come to me directly if you're confused about the schedule." And just like that, the whole room shifted. The air tightened.

I clenched my jaw. I knew the smart move was to let it go. To stay quiet. But that's not me. "Why not?" I said it, and the silence that followed was terrifying. Like a basketball thrown on an empty court. Slowly bouncing down to a roll.

He slowly stood up. At first, I avoided his glance. But eventually, I mustered up enough courage to lock eyes with his. He looked down at me, "Excuse me?"

Every part of my body was tense and straining. But I ignored it. "One of our core values is to 'Come Together.' How are we supposed to do that if we're told we can't ask each other questions?"

He shot his chair back, stormed across the room, and yanked my boss into a conference room.

A few minutes later, he came back out, calm and confident. He sat down without looking at me. "Travis, you should probably go see your boss."

No one looked up, and the only sound was my chair scraping the floor as I stood.

WHEN THE SYSTEM FAILS, NOBODY ELSE SEES IT, AND YOU HAVE TO FIND YOUR OWN WAY IN.

24

THE ACCESS

The clock was ticking. Five minutes left. Five minutes to convince the most powerful person in the company to grant me access to change something no one else seemed worried about yet. But I saw it coming. The engineers were already grumbling. Workarounds were already popping up. I could feel the same disaster unfolding, the same one I had *just* experienced at Faraday Future. And if I didn't stop it now, we'd be drowning in it for months.

I took a breath. "Can I please have admin access to the PLM system?"

He looked at his watch, probably to estimate how much time he had to soften the blow.

One of the hardest parts of joining Rivian was always worrying about who else they would hire from Faraday Future. On the upside? I knew who the rock stars were, the people I could count on when I needed help fast. But I also knew exactly who to be weary of. I'd spent the last six months at Faraday Future untangling the mess that some of the folks from the IT team had left behind. It'd been brutal, so I was always on alert.

The executive team at Faraday Future had pulled me off my regular battery work and put me in charge of a task force to figure out why we couldn't pay our suppliers. That task force dug deep for months as we traced every problem down to the root. And in the end, the problem had been clear as day. Some IT folks had set up the company's data management systems with oversimplified processes that didn't match the actual needs of the business. It was a total mismatch, and it had paralyzed the company. And while the task force had gotten closer and closer to nailing down this cause, those same people in IT had started quitting the company. One by one. Quietly. So the people who'd made the mess were gone before it could be fixed. And so, for six months straight, I'd doubled up—battery engineer by title, data management systems fixer by necessity—patching and rebuilding the company's data management systems piece by piece with a small team.

So when I'd joined Rivian and started spotting the same exact patterns in the data management system? My gut said the same folks were probably doing it again. I'd brought it up to my boss. He'd nodded and said he'd keep an eye on it but told me to stay focused on battery work. He didn't want to lose me to IT problems. Fine.

But by late 2019, I'd learned something that had stopped me cold: Rivian had hired the *exact same people* to build out the data management systems. Which meant Rivian had pivoted into the *same* software we'd used at Faraday Future. And right on cue, the engineers around me had started to feel it. Their frustration became palpable. You could hear it in the halls; gripes, jokes, and plans for workarounds. I knew that feeling. I'd lived it before. And I knew exactly where it would lead. It was the same mess playing out all over again. It was like I'd traveled back in time. And I knew what was coming.

I had only two choices: watch the same mess unfold again, knowing how bad it would get, or stop it before it spiraled.

I had to intervene. Obviously. But I couldn't waste any time. I owed the effort of hyper-efficiency for my boss's sake. So I'd sent an urgent email to the Chief Operating Officer for the company, asking for a meeting. I titled it something like *'Imminent threat to the company's survival'*. I'd figured that might get his attention.

He'd replied within minutes, and we were on the calendar for the next day.

When we sat down in the conference room, I barely opened my mouth before he held up a hand. "Thanks for flagging this. Really appreciate how much you're looking out for the company. But before we get to your thing, can I ask you something first?"

I nodded, ready for anything.

"I'm hearing bad things about the battery module line. Why can't we build these faster?"

I blinked. I was the lead engineer for the battery module by this point. I knew every millimeter, every snag, every delay. But I hadn't expected to be asked about that. "Uh, yeah," I started, scrambling. "We've got seven open issues right now." I laid it all out, calculating the correct things to hide to protect my boss from sabotage as I went along. It was exhausting.

He asked follow-ups, probing. I answered. He poked again. I explained again. I'd come prepared, sharp, focused. But as the minutes dragged on, it hit me: my issue was slipping away. He wasn't really there to listen.

Finally, after nearly twenty minutes, he seemed satisfied, like he'd squeezed what he needed out of me. He glanced at his watch, seemingly impatient to get somewhere else. "Alright," he said. "So, what's the problem you wanted to talk about?"

He couldn't stop looking at his phone, and I was almost in panic mode. My body was shaking, but I tried to tell myself I was fine and pushed on anyway. "I worked with a lot of the same IT folks here who I also worked with at Faraday, and we—"

"Who, exactly?"

I listed names. He waved me on, barely listening, eyes glazing. He had no idea who they were. Still, I kept going. "We ran a task force to figure out why Faraday couldn't pay its suppliers, and—"

"Who else was on that task force?"

I froze. The NDA. I knew what I could share, and what I couldn't. And the business management firm that had helped me on the task force was off-limits. Yet now, mid-sentence, I was realizing just how much I actually couldn't say.

I glanced at my watch. Two minutes left. So I just jumped straight to the point. "The CTO placed people on that task force under me. We figured out the core problem was an oversimplified data management system that was hastily stood up. The same people who built that are now building the same version here at Rivian. They disagreed with my findings. I know exactly how to fix what's coming, but it's too much to explain right now."

I took a quick breath. "Can I please have admin access to the PLM system? I'll just fix it and show you the results after. I can even do it in a sandbox."

He glanced at his watch again and mumbled something noncommittal. Then just left.

The realization slapped me hard. He'd used that entire meeting to serve his own agenda, and he'd gotten what he wanted. While I didn't get anything.

My head buzzed. My stomach churned. I felt disgusted, used, and stupid. There I was, a PhD chemist working as a battery engineer, trying to tell a veteran automotive executive that I knew more about data management systems than he did. Of course this is how it ended. How could I have been dumb enough to expect anything else?

Two days later, I was back at it. As if it had never happened. If anything, I felt more emboldened. I reasoned, *It can't get any worse. Nobody will make me feel worse than that.* So now all that was left was to find the shortest path remaining open. I'd started at the top. Now, I'd just work down the chain.

I asked my boss who had admin access to the PLM system. He told me. He didn't ask why. He knew by now that if he didn't tell me, I'd find out anyway, so it wasn't worth pretending I wouldn't. Then, I emailed every single one of them.

They all ignored me. All, that is, except for one. Thankfully, there's always one.

"I'm really curious to hear more about what you experienced. We've got some folks on the IT team here pushing some frustrating ideas and concepts, and nobody else seems to see it. Want to chat?"

We hopped on a call and talked for over an hour. He knew exactly what I was talking about; he was in the thick of it. He was drowning in the same mess I'd cleaned up at Faraday. He was exhausted, burned out, and desperate for someone to finally listen, just as I had been.

So I listened. And encouraged him. I let him vent, let him get it all out. And when he was done, I tried again. "Want to give me admin access? I'll fix it. If it blows up, you can blame me."

He laughed, but his voice was tight. "No way man. I'd get fired. First question would be, 'Who gave Travis access?' And I've got a family to feed, man."

I exhaled. I saw it so clearly now. I'd been in his shoes, buried, unseen, begging for backup. And now, I was the one on the outside, pleading to help. He was right. I couldn't put him in that position.

We wrapped up the call. I wished him luck. Then I went back on the offensive. I sent meeting requests to his boss. And that boss's boss. No bites.

Weeks passed. I hadn't quit. Instead, I'd built slide decks and sent more meeting requests. I kept talking about it to anyone who would listen. My boss started pushing too, raising the alarm with his higher-ups. Still, nothing. There were too many fires to fight. There was too much noise in the day-to-day. Nobody had the time, or the energy, to stop the mess from spreading. But it was still on my radar.

So one day, when I got an email from that friend—the one with PLM admin access—I opened it right away.

"Dear Travis, it's been a pleasure working with you. My time here has come to an end. My last day will be—"

I stopped reading. Heart racing, I yanked out my phone and fired off a text as fast as I could type. *"Wait! Before you go—can I PLEASE have admin access?"* I could have sworn I saw he was already texting me back before I'd even sent it.

"No." And a beat later. *"Of course not."*

But I knew him. And this 'no,' it wasn't like the others. I felt it in my gut as I stared at the message.

Voices from the phone meeting I was still in the middle of pushed through my thoughts, but I hung up and opened the PLM software instead. *No way. No. Freaking. Way.* After a few clicks, the screen shifted. The admin menu unfurled. I had access. Full access. My jaw dropped.

I spun around. Eyes wide, I looked at my boss. "I need to cancel all of my meetings for the rest of the week. Before anyone notices."

His eyebrows shot up. He glanced at my screen—eyes widening too—then threw his hands up to cover his face and backed away. "Nope. Nope. I don't want to know. I didn't see anything."

Well, with that settled, I cracked my knuckles and got to work. And as I did, something clicked. The real problem had never been those people in IT. Or the executive who'd ignored me. Or even the access itself. The real problem was that no one had the bandwidth to see the mess forming until it was too late.

That's why I'd been ignored. That's why my boss hid his face. They didn't have the energy to fight another fire. And that's why it had to be me. The fire, the chaos, the shame; this was the exact kind of mess I'd trained for.

And every stupid question I'd ever asked had prepared me.

WHEN YOU
ALREADY
KNOW THE
ANSWER, BUT
YOU KNOW
YOU HAVE TO
ASK ANYWAY.

25

THE HOPE

I was sure I'd said everything I needed to. He knew how much this meant to me. He knew the stakes. But I couldn't help myself; I had to add one more push. "Before you answer," I said carefully, "please know that this is incredibly important to me. I *really* want to do this." I let it hang there for a moment. Then I asked the only question that mattered: "Can I *please* do this?"

It was late 2020, and I was completely fried. Burned out in every way. The COVID-19 pandemic was still raging, but I'd been back in the office alongside the skeleton crew of the other essential workers since mid-May. I was 'essential.' And that was cool. For about a week. But that whole summer bled together into one big, messy mass of time.

I was the guy doing *everything*. Receiving packages for people who couldn't. Boxing other packages up again and shipped them out. Mopping floors, hauling trash, and building battery modules—and tearing them apart. And yet I kept showing up. Because what else could I do? I designed new parts and closed issue after issue on the manufacturing line in the Midwest. I got used to doing it all with a mask on and because most of the company was remote, I was tethered to my phone, bouncing from meeting to meeting while running around doing the physical work.

I needed something to change. Badly. A sabbatical. A reset. Anything.

The worst part wasn't the work. It was knowing that I was the only one on the team showing up for so long, every single day, no matter what. There were maybe eighty people on our team by this point. And only *one* of them lived farther away from the office than I did. At least thirty people I talked to daily lived just a few miles away from the office. And yet, somehow, I was the only one commuting. Some of them had pre-existing health conditions, which made sense. But I *knew* many of them didn't. They just wanted to work from home. In their PJ's.

Most mornings I'd stumble into the office on autopilot: blank, numb, and already exhausted. The coffee in my hand was often lukewarm, but I couldn't remember brewing it. My phone would buzz with another slew of texts: *"Hey, can you grab my package at the front desk?" "Or, wait, he's waiting out front because nobody's at the front desk." "When you grab it, can you measure the thickness from datum A and get a weight and…"* I would read as long as I could before I'd have to slam my phone down and grit my teeth.

And this day marked the tenth time I had to in the last few days. The pleasantries by this point were gone. None of that, "When you can" or "If it's not a bother."

A week had passed since I'd last seen my daughter awake. A month since I'd had a real conversation with Emily. And months—so many months—since I'd had a full night's sleep. I wasn't an engineer anymore. I wasn't even a dad. I was just ... there. Roaming an empty office by day and an empty home by night, a ghost floating through my own life. Alone.

My phone lit up again. An email: *Meeting request - Intellectual Property Team.* Before I even registered it, a warmth pushed up from my chest into my face. I was smiling, and I couldn't stop my eyes from welling up at the first real spark of joy I'd felt all month.

There was one thing, only one thing, that never failed to light me up, no matter how bad things got in those days. Any time I heard from the IP team, whether it was an email, a phone call, or a text, my whole world got brighter. Didn't matter what it was; a random check-in to see if I had any new ideas, a request to review a patent draft, even something as dry as weighing in on a lawsuit about our battery portfolio. The second their name popped up, I'd light up like a kid on Christmas.

I was good at inventing. And I loved it. I felt like it was the thing I was meant to do. So, I accepted the meeting without even reading past the title and stopped thinking about it. I intentionally forgot about it so my calendar could surprise me later.

I did that a lot those days.

My phone buzzed again. Then it started ringing. *Damn it.* I raced to get the package.

The surprise came when I was *really* in the thick of a big redesign. I was one of the company's top experts on thermal runaway. I was the lead for the redesign. One of them, anyway. Yet, I didn't prepare for the IP meeting at all. I never did. Never needed to. Inventing was the easiest thing in the world. So when we kicked off the meeting, and the IP engineer thanked me and introduced the company's General Counsel, I thought, *Maybe I should have read the meeting invite.*

I apologized for coming unprepared, but the GC shushed me. "Oh, please, it's fine. We owe you thanks! Thank you for sending some more engineers our way with patentable ideas for us to pursue!"

I grinned. "Of course! I love helping you guys and the team. It's a triple win. You stay busy, the company's IP portfolio grows, and those engineers get to beef up their resumes."

"That's exactly why I wanted to talk to you," he said. "You seem to have a pretty good feel for how to spot and manage Intellectual Property. Have you ever thought about making it your full-time career?"

I laughed it off. "I mean, I've thought about it, but I'm way too busy. There's no way I could juggle all this and go back to school for a law degree."

He nodded. "Totally fair. Well, in a previous life, I introduced a role called the *IP Liaison*. Basically, I picked an engineer who would spend half their time on IP management and the other half on their regular engineering work. It gave them a chance to really test the waters before committing long-term. And if they liked it, we'd help them transition fully into IP, either as an engineer or an attorney."

My eyes went wide. "Whoa. That sounds incredible."

He smiled. "Well, we're thinking of launching the program here at Rivian. And a lot of people brought up your name. So, we were wondering, would you be interested in being our first pilot candidate?"

It hit me like a freight train. I'd spent so much time fixing other people's problems, I'd completely forgotten what it felt like for someone to help me with mine.

I sat there, stunned, before I finally managed to push out, "Yes. Absolutely. Thank you so much for thinking of me."

The GC grinned. "Yeah. I was told you'd probably say that."

I started to thaw. My eyes welled up as the weight of every single late night, every sacrifice, every ounce of exhaustion lifted off of me. I could taste the freedom.

Suddenly, I found my mind back in grad school. In that crumbling apartment, shared with the rat. I could see my past self, sobbing, alone, hopeless. And I reached through time to hug him. *Look. You did it. You found your path. I'm so proud of you for not giving up.*

All the missed time with Emily, with my daughter Lucy, I let it go. I'd worked my ass off, and I'd earned my reward. My sabbatical had arrived. I could barely believe it; I *had* to grab it.

"So ... how do we make it official?"

He smiled. "Simple. We just need to loop in your boss and get his approval."

And just like that, the weight came crashing back down on me.

I kept my face as steady as I could, thanked him for the opportunity, and ended the call. I had to cry for real.

I knew this feeling. It felt exactly like NASA all over again. Only this time, it hadn't even happened yet. And my gut was already telling me this would go the same way. *Don't bother.*

But I wasn't about to listen to that kind of talk. I'd give it my best shot regardless of the risk. So I would always remember this moment. If it would be a no, it would be a no after I gave it everything I had.

I took a full day to prepare. Then another. I called Emily from the office, rehearsing with her, over and over, until I could say it without shaking. Confidently. And finally, I set the meeting with my boss.

When I walked in, I stuck to the script like glue. "I wanted to talk to you about an opportunity that came up." I laid out everything. I told him how burned out I was. How much this could help, not just me but the team. How I thought the role might even give me some flexibility; more time with the family, a way to recharge. And I stressed that it was just half my time. I said we could collaborate closely to figure out exactly how to split it—week by week, day by day, whatever worked best. "But it can only happen if you approve. And before you answer, please know this is incredibly important to me. I *really* want to do this." I let it sit for a second. Then I added, "Can I please do this?"

I held my breath. Hoping, just for a second, that maybe he'd see what I saw. That he'd throw me the lifeline. But I saw it. The hesitation. The fear. And I knew it was over.

He started talking. But I couldn't hear it. Couldn't process it. I just sat there, trying not to break down, watching the door slam shut. He didn't mince words. It was a no. Because I was 'too valuable to the team.'

I didn't even need to think about who to call first. Nate. He wasn't just my closest friend I'd met at Rivian. He was Rivian's other prolific inventor. Together, his name or mine showed up on 30% of the company's entire publicly known patent portfolio. We were unstoppable inventors. A strong duo.

He had left Rivian a while ago for something new. But before that, he'd taught me everything I knew about inventing. He didn't just understand my love for it, he *felt* it. Lived it, the same way I did. So if anyone could understand how crushed I felt in that moment, it was Nate.

I called him immediately, and we met up that night. Wrung out and raw, I told him everything. He let me vent, nodding along, quiet and steady. And vent I did, until I had nothing left.

He asked how Emily was. How my daughter Lucy was. When I said I didn't know, he smacked his lips. He put his glass down and leaned in to clap me on the shoulder. And said the one thing I never thought he would: "How'd you like to come help me build some airplanes?"

I laughed.

He didn't. "The office is a mile from your house. We work mostly 9:00 to 5:00. No weekends." Perhaps I should have been grateful for the offer, but instead, I got mad. I didn't need more hope. Not when I was too exhausted to get my hopes up again. Then he finished with what he *knew* would hook me. "Lots of white space. Lots of room for new ideas."

He left after that, to go on a date, and I drove home, crying for my lost chance the whole way back. But later that night, I couldn't help myself. I opened up my phone and started researching how airplanes work.

WHEN YOU'RE AT YOUR LOWEST, SOMETIMES ALL YOU NEED IS A HUG FROM A TINY HUMAN.

26

THE HUG

I'd failed. And I knew it the instant the words left my mouth. Heart pounding, voice shaking, I forced out what little I had left. "What can I do to make it right?" I was kneeling, eyes stinging, scared to hear her response.

It was a few days before Christmas 2024, and everything—my body, my mind, my spirit—was crumbling. I had a fever. My whole body throbbed. Every breath hurt. My head, my throat, my chest were raw and ragged.

That morning, my sense of taste and smell had vanished, so the eggnog I'd been waiting for all year became nothing but cold sludge.

I stared at the tiny pile of presents under the tree, a physical, undeniable reminder of how badly I was failing. We'd run out of savings weeks ago. I'd been laid off in early September, and another rejection email had just landed, another slammed door. The cars were sitting on empty. The mortgage was overdue. And we only had cash in the bank because my parents had floated us a bridge loan.

Every day I told myself, *I just need one yes. Just one. That's all it takes.* Then, Stella, our youngest daughter, sneezed without covering her mouth, and I lost it.

"SEE, STELLA? You didn't cover your mouth! That's why we're all sick, because you can't be bothered to COVER YOUR MOUTH!" My voice rose, sharp and bitter. "None of you *ever* get sick when I do! But the *second* one of you are sick? I'm doomed! WHY? I work *so hard* to keep you all healthy. WHY does nobody care if I get sick? Why can't ANYONE in this house think about anyone but themself?!"

Emily, just as sick, if not worse, glared at me. "Dude. She's three."

Stella disappeared toward her room, quietly crying. She knew better than to make noise when I was like this.

I grabbed the dishes and scrubbed like my life depended on it. I just wanted to control one thing. I wanted a job. I wanted to call the mortgage company with good news. I wanted to stop feeling like a failure. By the third dish, I paused and just resigned myself to the universe.

Fine, I thought. *I'll just give up trying to get anything done tonight. It's useless. I'm useless.*

That last rejection had hit me hard. I'd wanted it so badly, it hurt. And I'd really thought I'd had it. I'd been the runner-up. Second place. I'd thrown *so much* into those interviews. And with that rejection, we were going to run out of money. I'd have to apply for a loan. We'd probably have to sell our house, pull the girls out of school, and move somewhere else.

As I picked up and continued to scrub that third dish, it start creeping in. The thought. The life insurance policy.

For a second, it almost seemed rational. Clean. A single decision that could fix everything. Then, just as fast, I recognized it for what it was. The invisible hand. I was fabricating shame, I had to lean into it. I had to push through. I had to ask a stupid question. And as soon as I realized that, I could only think of one thing.

Stella; the look on her face. What had I done?

I dropped the dish so fast, it almost broke. It started as a sprint, but I slowed to a brisk walk to her room. Before I opened the door, I heard Emily in there, helping the kids get changed into their pajamas. They were all joking and laughing as if nothing had happened. As if I hadn't yelled. They'd moved on in minutes.

But I hadn't.

Stella was putting her shirt on when I asked, "Can I talk to you?"

She rolled her eyes. "Okay, Daddy."

I took a deep breath. "I shouldn't have snapped at you like that. That was wrong." She rolled her eyes again. I kept going. "Daddy's just really upset right now. I'm having a really hard time, but it was wrong for me to take that out on you. I'm so sorry. I love you so much." And I knew I had to ask something. Something I was afraid to. So I asked the only thing that I was truly afraid of what the answer might be. "What can I do to make it right?"

She rolled her eyes again. And, without taking those precious little fingers out of her mouth, the fingers she puts there to soothe herself, she said, "It's okay, Daddy. You can go do whatever you want."

So, I asked for a hug. And as we hugged, everything—the weight, the failure, the shame—lifted.

She knew. She knew I wasn't the things I said or did when I was breaking. She knew I was Daddy, and that I always would be. And in that moment, I knew it too.

> Stupid questions aren't about learning.
> And they're *definitely* not about
> stupidity. They're about connection,
> about reaching for understanding with
> others instead of retreating into shame.

I'd spent years pondering stupid questions; the power they hold, the pathways they show us, the discomfort they demand. But this moment made one thing abundantly clear: knowing their power wasn't enough. I had to do more.

The next day, I sat down and started writing this book. In the hopes that maybe, just maybe, it could help someone else choose courageous connection over silent shame.

WHEN YOU REALIZE YOU NEVER NEEDED PERMISSION IN THE FIRST PLACE.

27

THE BEGINNING

I spent many years thinking I was alone. That I was the *only one* who froze when I had a question. I thought I was the only one whose face flushed hot, whose stomach twisted, whose mind went blank. The only one who thought, *Don't ask that. You'll sound stupid.*

But I'm not alone. And neither are you.

There are times when it takes courage to be curious. Your times will be different from mine, but all stupid questions are beautiful in the same way. That's been the quiet truth all along.

Stupid questions are honest questions
you're shamed for asking

Everywhere I've worked—in every classroom, meeting, late-night conversation—I've seen it. We're all haunted by the same invisible hand. The one that pushes yours down. The shame might have been planted there by someone else. Or maybe it only ever existed in your head. Or maybe it hasn't been planted at all yet. But we're all carrying around questions we're too afraid to ask, questions we want to ask but think we can't. Big ones. Small. Ones we *never* ask because we're convinced we should know the answer. Ones we pretend don't matter but we can't stop thinking about. Ones we'll ask later when we're safe. Questions that eat us up inside.

And that shame? It keeps us stuck. It keeps us small. And *it will continue to* unless we opt for something else. Unless we choose to challenge the status quo. And believe that stupid questions exist. That they can change everything. That when you ask with courage—when you push through that heat in your face, the knot in your stomach, the voice in your head that says *don't*—that's when everything starts to change.

That's how we grow. That's when things open up. And the only way to make it through to the other side—to break free—is to ask anyway. To speak up, even when your voice shakes. To push past the heat, the fear, the shame. To risk sounding like an idiot to find out what's *actually* true.

It's not always easy. Sometimes we overshoot into more shame than we should have. Sometimes we think we can handle more than we actually can. Sometimes, yeah, it hurts. Sometimes people roll their eyes. Sometimes it feels like no one's listening. But sometimes, we find something better than our wildest expectations, a new path we wouldn't have seen otherwise, a chance to grow in a way you didn't know you needed.

Whether you're a student asking your first hard question; a seasoned professor surprised by a student leading you into new territory; a colleague desperate for a reprieve; a boss navigating a career transition;

another boss afraid to lose your star player; a parent learning alongside your toddler; or just a person just trying to figure it out as you go, *You belong here.*

In this world of Courageous Curiosity, a world where stupid questions aren't the end of the conversation, they're the beginning. So if you've been holding back, hesitating, worrying, wondering whether you belong in this messy, uncertain space? You do. *You always have.*

The invitation is open. It's up to you to choose what you'll do with it. You know where I stand. I've been toughing it out in this world for years. So, what are you waiting for? Come on in, and Ask Anyway to your heart's desire.

WHEN YOU
EMBARK ON
SOMETHING
AS BIG AND
SCARY AS
WRITING A
BOOK, YOUR
COMMUNITY
SHOWS UP.

THE ACKNOWLEDGEMENTS

The first people I'd like to thank are all the advisors, mentors, and bosses who have put up with me throughout my entire checkered education & career. I fully acknowledge I am remarkably different and awkward in so many ways, and trying to take on the task of managing or advising me probably felt kind of overwhelming. I often can't keep up with the reasoning behind my own thoughts. I can only imagine how difficult the same task was for you.

Thank you for mustering up as much patience as you could. Through all the struggles I've had, I've noticed every sigh and deep breath as you tried your best. Thank you. Our common struggle formed the basis for most of this book.

To the Cournoyer clan, Mom, Dad, Jarod and Nicole. Thank you for always answering the phone, no matter how late I called or how many times I forgot about the time difference. Thank you for being patient, for listening, and for holding space every time I called home overwhelmed or excited by what I learned while writing this book. You've always been my safe place to ask stupid questions, even before I knew how much courage that required.

Thank you for giving me everything I ever needed to find my own path forward. I love you all more than words can say.

To Keidi Keating, the master wordsmith who copy edited this manuscript to its completion. Thank you for helping me craft this narrative from something that kind of made sense into something that would land with those it's meant for.

To Mike Pietrobon, the creative wizard who designed the book in all of its forms. Thank you for convincing me to self-publish this manuscript to get it out to the world faster. Thank you for designing such a beautiful book in every format.

I will forever be grateful for your guidance and support as I navigated my way into this publishing world. I greatly look forward to seeing where it goes from here.

To Ian Rye, for graciously raising your hand to be a beta reader for one of the earliest and least sensical versions of this book. And for delivering feedback that was so impactful I deleted almost everything I had originally sent your way. Your recommendation to rewrite basically the entire book was taken to heart.

Thank you for pointing out how confused I was about what I was trying to say so that I could get to clarity. Your comment about who would pick this book up and how I could more intentionally write it for them means the world to me, and I agonized over it for hours on end until it finally clicked. I hope it ended up being a book you'd pick up on the shelf.

To my first-ever life coach Michele Young, who's always been more like a sister-in-law than anything else. Thank you for helping me get unstuck long enough to get this book on the page. Thank you for being my most involved beta reader making it through multiple iterations of the text, patiently wading through the muck of my initial thoughts, and pushing me firmly yet kindly to "find the point." I finally did.

I will forever be grateful for your teaching me how to 'frame my focus', not just in writing, but in life. Thank you.

To my best friend Nate Wynn, the first person throughout my entire career who truly made me feel like I fit in. Thank you for making fun of me that day we met at Rivian. Thank you for not giving up on me even though I was the idiot who didn't know what I squared R was. Thank you for showing me how to discover a love and passion for invention (I promise I'll catch up to you one day!) Thank you for teaching me how to take measured risks in ways that ignite change without overwhelming others.

Thank you for being the first person I ever told about this book, and for patiently listening while I stumbled through trying to explain it before I fully understood it myself. Thank you for reading the first full draft of this book, during what was probably the busiest time of your life, to gently point its publication in a useful way that wouldn't violate any of the many NDA's that you and I have signed.

Thank you for letting me stand next to you at your wedding to celebrate such a huge part of your life. And above all, thank you for helping me learn how to believe in myself.

I am forever grateful we met. Thank you.

To Emily, my wife. Thank you for seeing who I was before I could see it myself, and for loving me long before I figured out how to love myself. Thank you for enduring countless stupid questions, asked both too early and too late, and for teaching me what real patience looks like. Thank you for holding our family together during all those times I couldn't, for quietly shouldering the burdens I didn't notice, and for always having faith in who I could become.

You have carried me through the darkest moments, patiently waiting for me to just…walk on out. I could never have written a word of this book without your unwavering strength, support, and love. This book is as much yours as it is mine. Thank you. You are my favorite person.

To my daughters, Lucy and Stella. Thank you for working so hard to have good listening ears. Thank you for understanding all the times Daddy had to go away to Northern California for work while I was writing this book. And thank you for understanding that, even when I was home with you in Southern California on the weekends, I still needed to do some writing to get this book finished. I'm done now! So, as promised, let's go to Disneyland!

www.ingramcontent.com/pod-product-compliance
Lightning Source LLC
Chambersburg PA
CBHW011221120626
46545CB00010B/3098